The Black Prince at Crécy

TEN BOYS.
FROM HISTORY

BY
KATE DICKINSON SWEETSER
AUTHOR OF
"TEN BOYS FROM DICKENS" "TEN GREAT ADVENTURERS"
"BOOK OF INDIAN BRAVES" ETC.

ILLUSTRATED BY
GEORGE ALFRED WILLIAMS

Fredonia Books
Amsterdam, The Netherlands

Ten Boys from History

by
Kate Dickinson Sweetser

ISBN: 1-58963-599-X

Copyright © 2001 by Fredonia Books

Reprinted from the 1817 edition

Fredonia Books
Amsterdam, The Netherlands
http://www.fredoniabooks.com

All rights reserved, including the right to reproduce this book, or portions thereof, in any form.

In order to make original editions of historical works available to scholars at an economical price, this facsimile of the original edition of 1817 is reproduced from the best available copy and has been digitally enhanced to improve legibility, but the text remains unaltered to retain historical authenticity.

PREFACE

In this small volume the boys of many lands and races whose stories are told, have been selected not because they later became famous men, although some of them did, but because each one achieved something noteworthy as a boy. And in each boy's character, whether historic or legendary, courage was the marked trait. For this reason it is hoped that their stories will prove stimulating to some who read them.

K. D. S.

CONTENTS

	PAGE
STEPHEN AND NICHOLAS: BOY CRUSADERS	11
PETER OF HAARLEM: THE BOY WHO SAVED HIS COUNTRY	45
DAVID: THE SHEPHERD BOY	55
LOUIS SEVENTEENTH: THE BOY KING WHO NEVER REIGNED	91
EDWARD THE BLACK PRINCE: THE BOY WARRIOR	131
TYRANT TAD: THE BOY IN THE WHITE HOUSE	145
HUGH OF LINCOLN: THE BOY CHORISTER	169
DAVID FARRAGUT: THE BOY MIDSHIPMAN	179
MOZART: THE BOY MUSICIAN	197

ILLUSTRATIONS

	PAGE
THE BLACK PRINCE AT CRÉCY . . .	*Frontispiece*
DAVID AND GOLIATH	55
TYRANT TAD AND ABRAHAM LINCOLN . . .	145
DAVID FARRAGUT	179

STEPHEN AND NICHOLAS
Boy Crusaders

TEN BOYS FROM HISTORY

STEPHEN AND NICHOLAS: Boy Crusaders

> "To the sea of fools
> Led the path of the children."
> *Old Epigram.*

JUST a word about the Crusades, or Holy Wars, before we begin our story.

A war is generally a conflict between nations, countries, or individuals, for possession of land or a throne, but the Holy Wars were not such. They were expeditions made by those Christians who were determined to rescue the Sepulchre, or tomb, of Christ and the City of Jerusalem, from the rule of unbelievers.

For eighty-eight years Christian kings ruled in Palestine, then all the land was conquered by the Mohammedans, except a few cities, and the Christians sent out another, and still another, and another expedition to subdue the enemy, but all were useless. The Holy City and the Holy Sepulchre were still in the hands of infidels, who persecuted the pilgrims who visited the Holy Tomb; and the Christians sent a heart-rending cry to all Europe for help, but Europe was slow to answer the appeal, and it was several years after Pope Innocent ordered a new Crusade, before an army departed for the scene of conflict.

It was during this interval that the Children's Crusade or Holy War, took place—of which we are about to read.

But first let us go back to the city of Chartres, on the 25th day of April, 1212, when a surging crowd of men and women is filling every street and by-way of the quaint city.

What are the crowds watching so eagerly? A procession of priests and laymen, carrying banners and black-draped crosses, and chanting in solemn unison as they march.

It is the day of the celebration in Chartres of the "Black Crosses," an old church ceremony instituted centuries before, by Gregory the Great, during the ravages of the Plague, but now celebrated as an appeal to the people to free Jerusalem and the Holy Tomb from the hands of the infidels.

The solemn ranks of the procession move slowly through the streets of Chartres, carrying black-draped symbols of a Saviour's death, chanting deep-toned litanies, and that the old ceremony has lost none of its emotional power is shown by the tears and silence of the watching throngs, while among all the crowd none is more profoundly stirred than a slender shepherd lad from the neighbouring town of Cloyes, who is seeing the ceremony for the first time.

Agile as such a lad should be, and sturdy in consequence of his out-of-door life, Stephen, for that was his name, found it an easy matter to breast the surging tide of spectators following the procession, to slip in where he could to best advantage watch the solemn ceremonies, to stand

STEPHEN AND NICHOLAS

without fatigue while he drank in all the emotional thrill of the day.

The shrouded crosses, the appeals for rescue of an entombed Christ in the hands of an infidel enemy, the tears and cries of the crowds, worked on the impressionable shepherd lad, unaccustomed to aught but life with his flocks, worked on him so powerfully that he was hot with a desire to rush to Jerusalem and expel the hated Mohammedans from that land and city, once blessed by the living presence of Jesus, and hallowed by the possession of his tomb.

So filled with enthusiasm was Stephen that his burning cheeks and glowing eyes told the tale to an observant priest, who to accomplish his own end, kept close watch of the boy, spoke to him, making inquiries as to his name and occupation, and then decided to make him a tool of destiny.

But of this Stephen knew nothing. Filled with thoughts of what he had seen and heard, at evening he walked slowly towards his home in the little village of Cloyes, walking less on solid earth than on a cloud of dreams and desires, and from that moment he was never again the contented shepherd lad, son of the peasant of Cloyes. He was alive with new emotions now, and as he wandered on the hillside with his flock he was in imagination the hero of daring deeds, taking part in such pictured scenes as his excited fancy could conjure up, until at last, he was in a state of mind suited to any enterprise, prepared to believe any story, however improbable, to accept any life except that of his own monotonous peasant existence.

While in this mood there came to him on his hillside, several days later, a stranger in the dress of a pilgrim, returned, as he at first said, from Palestine. He was on his way to a distant home and in need of food.

TEN BOYS FROM HISTORY

Only too eagerly did Stephen share with him such food as he had, asking in return to be told of the wonders of the Holy Land and of the daring deeds of the heroes who had fallen there in battle. The stranger readily complied with this request and poured into the boy's credulous ears tales well calculated to thrill and excite his already inflamed fancy. Then, watching Stephen closely as he spoke, the stranger said with solemn earnestness:

"But this is not all I have to tell, my lad. There is work for you to do,—for you, the Lord's anointed, his chosen apostle, and in the name of Christ and his Holy Cross, I bid you arise and do his will."

"Work?—for me? From whom comes this message?"

Stephen's eyes were lit with the fire of excited desire and his voice trembled with emotion.

Very slowly the answering words fell from his companion's lips:

"The message is brought by him who sends it. Behold, lad, the Christ of history and of truth! *I* bid you arise—rouse up the youth of our land! Lead them to that Holy Sepulchre! As prophet and as leader, go thou where they shall follow, and bring to pass that which nobles and soldiers have failed to accomplish. Go lad—go!"

Stephen's breath came in quick gasps—his eyes were like coals of fire as he sank on his knees, crying:

"Oh bless me—bless me—I will go—Lord, I will go!"

A hand was laid gently on his head as the deep voice said, "In the name of Jesus, lad—in the name of the Crucified, lead thou thy troops to victory. Across the land, across the sea, lead them to victory!" Then in a less impassioned tone, the stranger added, "I leave with you a letter to the king of France. Haste thou to him with this proof of thy divine mission and he will aid thee in thy enterprise. In the name of Jesus, lad, arise and go!"

A letter was pressed into Stephen's hand. He heard retreating footsteps, and before he had gained his composure and risen to his feet, his divine guest was gone. He was alone with his straying flock, not sure except for the letter, whether he had had a vision or a visitor.

And how was he to know, innocent peasant lad, of an ignorant and superstitious ancestry, brought up on miraculous tales of saints and seers, that the Christ of his visit was no other than that priest whose attention Stephen had attracted by his emotion at Chartres, who with crafty keenness had chosen the peasant boy to carry out his purpose of arousing the youth of the land to undertake a new Crusade? How was Stephen, all aflame as he was, to be supposed to penetrate the priest's disguise, to realise his purpose, and throw off the thrill? He could not and he did not.

Leaving his flocks to ramble at will over the plains and neighbouring hills, with the divine letter clasped in his hand, Stephen ran homeward through the little village where he lived, past its dilapidated church, its quaint shops and rows of houses, over the old stone bridge by which the main street crosses the little river Loir, running in a southerly direction to join the beautiful Loire. The bridge is a pleasant place to linger on a summer day, and recalls many a historic memory of Joan of Arc, who once passed that way, on her way to Orleans—of Philip Augustus—of Richard Cœur-de-Lion—but on naught save his divine mission was the lad Stephen intent as he crossed the bridge on that April day.

Having reached home, he hastily called his parents from their labour, and gathering together such neighbours as could be summoned, he told of his talk with the Saviour, who had come to call him, Stephen, the shepherd boy, from tending his flocks, to rescue the Holy City and tomb from wicked hands, and in proof of the truth of his story he showed the letter from Jesus Christ to the King of France asking the king's aid for Stephen in his holy mission.

As I have said, this was an age of dense ignorance and superstition among the peasant classes. Those who had heard Stephen's tale were dumb with awe and wonder and doubted not its truth. Only his father spoke against the plan, mentioning his son's youth—commanding him to go back to his flocks. But to these commands Stephen turned a deaf ear, for was not he the Lord's anointed? Who could dictate to him, now that the Divine voice had spoken in accents clear and strong?

On the next day and the next, even until darkness fell over the little town, Stephen narrated his story in the market-place to ever-increasing audiences, telling that now when the defenders of the Holy Sepulchre were so few, and older and stronger Crusaders had failed to carry out their divine purpose by reason of the ravages of war and disease, God had revealed his plan to give the possession of Palestine to those children who should enlist in his holy cause.

"For the last time have we heard of defeat," cried Stephen. "Hereafter shall children show mailed warriors and proud barons how invulnerable are youths when God leads them!"

This cry stirred the youths of Cloyes profoundly, and they all rushed to enlist under the banner of Stephen and the Holy Cross, but the number was not large enough to satisfy Stephen's ambition. He was determined now to rouse all France and in consequence of that desire, he decided to leave his home and go to a town five miles north

STEPHEN AND NICHOLAS

of Paris—St. Denys, the great shrine of the land, where lie the bones of the martyr Dionysius, the object of countless pilgrimages, where to ever-changing crowds, he could preach his Crusade, and gain recruits for his army.

And so to St. Denys, Stephen of Cloyes went, in May of 1212. Dressed in his shepherd's clothes, for he had no others, with his crook in his hand and a little wallet by his side, he left quiet Cloyes for ever. With a heart throbbing with hope and excitement, he journeyed on, feeling neither fatigue nor fear, and as he went he preached his mission in towns and cities by the way, and ever the interest deepened in this lad who spoke with such burning eloquence, proclaiming himself God's chosen instrument to rescue the Holy Sepulchre, and everywhere he gained recruits. But even in Paris and Chartres, he did not linger long, being eager to reach St. Denys. At last he arrived there, and standing at the door of the historic church which contained the martyr's tomb, proclaimed his new Crusade to astonished crowds whom he fascinated by his unusual eloquence as he told the old story of the sufferings of the Christians in the Holy Land, telling it so simply and so vividly that his audiences were profoundly stirred, especially by Stephen's last and best appeal. He pointed to the Sepulchre of St. Denys, to which worshippers were thronging, and contrasted its condition with that of the Sepulchre of the Saviour, asking if his hearers would not help him make the Saviour's tomb as honoured and as free from disturbing influences as was that of the saint. He then read his letter to the king and asked if God's commands were to be disregarded, telling of his interview with Christ, and adding that after his day in Chartres, he had gone in search of his flocks and found them missing, but had later discovered them in a field of grain, from which he was about to drive them angrily, when they fell on their knees and begged his forgiveness. This, he said, with other signs, had led him to believe that he was truly God's anointed, even before he had been visited by Christ.

It may well be asked here how a lad scarcely over twelve years of age and born of the peasant class, could have suddenly become so eloquent—so capable of appealing to audiences, and the answer is not easy to give unless one thoroughly understands the spirit of that age in which Stephen lived—an age in which there was much high-coloured and stirring language used by the priests, language which appealed so strongly to an impressionable lad like Stephen, that he unconsciously took it for his own and made use of it; being often carried on the tide of his emotion, far beyond his own understanding of the words and thoughts he was uttering.

Immediately, he became the Saint of the day, and the martyr's bones were deserted by those who preferred to listen to the lad's stirring appeals. It is even reported that he worked miracles to support his own divine claim, and the enthusiasm to join his army grew daily more intense. As pilgrims went back to their homes they carried news of Stephen's Crusade to their children, who, filled with excitement, in turn passed the news on to their friends. And so the interest spread like a contagion throughout all parts of France, through Brittany, where the English ruled, through Normandy, recently added to Philip's domain, to Aquitaine and Provence, to Toulouse and peaceful Gascony. Whatever feuds their parents were engaged in, the children did not care, and were not interested in the wars for power. So while their elders were prevented from unity of action by the strife and political divisions of

STEPHEN AND NICHOLAS

the land, the young were one in feeling and in desire, and joined gleefully in Stephen's stirring cry:

"Long enough have you knights and warriors, so boastful and so honoured, been making your fruitless attempts to rescue the tomb of Christ! God can wait no longer! He is tired of your vain puny efforts. Stand back and let us, whom you despise, carry out his commission! He who calls can insure the victory, and we will show you what the children can do!"

Among the children who listened to Stephen's appeals, the more enterprising returned home determined to play a part in the Crusade only second to that of the Prophet, as Stephen was now called. Everywhere in France, they went through their home districts, begging their companions to join the Crusade, and it is probable that these children had much help from priests who sought in every way to inflame the youthful host, and to lead them on to concerted action.

As the army grew larger, the children formed into bands, and marched through towns and villages with all the pomp and display possible, despite much opposition from their parents, who saw with alarm that the excitement was growing daily more intense. The bands of recruits carried lighted candles, waving perfumed censers, and at the head of every band there marched a proud youth carrying the Oriflamme—a copy of the flag of the church, which was kept at St. Denys. The design of this banner was a red triple-tongued flame, symbolic of the tongues of fire that came down at Pentecost. This banner, like the colours of a regiment, was a symbol of honour, and an object of the young Crusader's devotion.

As the bands marched, they either sang hymns, such as had kept up the courage of previous Crusaders, or others composed on the spur of the moment by their fevered children's minds, and in all of the hymns came the refrain—"Lord, restore Christendom! Lord, restore to us the true and holy Cross!"

And too they adopted the watchword which for two centuries had rung through Asia. Crying, "God wills it!" children of all classes and conditions and ages, cast aside authority, and joined the army, and soon the movement became like the surge of a great wave, carrying the youth of France out on its dangerous tide—girls as well as boys—weak as well as strong—joining the forces.

Of course, the matter attracted the attention of the king, Philip Augustus, who at first, for political reasons, was inclined to favour the young Crusaders, but then seeing how serious the matter really was, and that if it were not suppressed it would bear away the youth of the land, to almost certain disaster, finally issued an edict or command that the children return to their homes.

Kings are too wise to pay any attention even to messages written by a divine hand, and there is no evidence to show that Philip was in any way influenced by the letter given to Stephen by his celestial visitor, and Philip's edict went forth, that there be an end to the uprising of the children.

But in vain was the edict, which the King did not attempt to enforce, in vain were all the commands and threats and pleas of parents and guardians. Stephen's Crusade had become an epidemic. If a lad were locked up that he might not join its ranks, he straightway sickened; some even died of pining; where commands were the only bar to freedom, the youths utterly disregarded them and ran away. So, after a few weeks of Stephen's inflamed preaching there was rebellion in many a before happy

STEPHEN AND NICHOLAS

household in France, agony in many a mother's heart, who saw her children leaving her, never, as her mother instinct told her, to return.

In the ranks of recruits were many noble youths, sons of counts and barons, who had from birth been brought up with knights and warriors who had won fame and honour in former Crusades, and who told glowing tales of the beauty and charm of the Holy Land to their children, and these were naturally thrilled at the thought of seeing such scenes and doing such deeds of valour, in gorgeous armour and on prancing steeds, for so did they picture themselves, as their fathers had done before them.

And there were others whose fathers had died in the Wars of the Cross, whose feverish dream was to make use of their father's honoured sword and shield and thus complete the work that Death had cut short. When these youths from the hills on which their homes stood, watched the processions passing with uplifted crosses and banners waving high, when they heard the songs and shouts of triumph, they could not be held back from joining the throng, and from their thousand homes they came to join the army, while higher and higher swelled the excitement, despite the opposition of king and clergy.

While Stephen was preaching at St. Denys, trying to gather his army together with all speed, tidings of the new Crusade were brought to a boy in a village near Cologne, a boy who had always been keenly interested in reading and hearing of the Crusades, and who was at once filled with a desire to follow the leadership of Stephen.

Nicholas, for that was this German lad's name, had a father who was both clever and ambitious. He knew the precocity of his son, and desiring to have the boy's talents bring him fame, and perhaps worldly benefits, worked on, the boy's young mind in every possible way, until Nicholas believed himself to be called of God to imitate the example of Stephen, and to go to Cologne and preach as Stephen was doing at St. Denys.

Old Cologne was a great and influential city, and at that time the religious centre of Germany, and there Nicholas went and preached, telling, and doubtless with much suggestion and help from his father, many marvellous tales of the cross of blazing light which had been his pledge of success in the Holy War. Now we hear him speaking in impassioned words by the door of the old Cathedral, now on a platform surrounded by his credulous audience, and again simply standing on the street corner telling his story, while like the widening ripples from a stone thrown into the still waters of a lake, widened the ripples of interest in the new Crusade among the German children.

For reasons politic, the Emperor suppressed the matter where he could, but in the vicinity of the Rhine and the neighbouring land of Burgundy, the mania spread like wildfire, and as in France, overcame all opposition, until in little over a month after the first preaching of Nicholas, his bands were ready to depart for the Holy Land, while Stephen, Prophet and leader in France, was still waiting for the completion of his army, recruits for which were ever pouring into St. Denys, and although Stephen had never seen Nicholas, it must have been anything but an easy matter for him to control his feelings and act as such a divinely appointed leader should, when he heard that Nicholas was ready to lead his forces on to victory, while he, Stephen, first called of God, was left behind.

But there was no help for it, and on a morning of early July, in 1212, the German bands were ready to march to glory. Most of them wore the long grey coat of the Crusader, with its Cross upon the right shoulder, which, with the addition of the palmer's staff they carried, and the broad-brimmed hat they wore, made a quaint and pleasing effect upon the childish figures—while it showed to great advantages the broad shoulders and fine figure of sturdy Nicholas, who was as different as possible in physique and temperament from high-strung sensitive Stephen.

Now the hour of their departure has come. The army of Nicholas is ready to start from Cologne—a great crowd of spectators surrounds them, watching their movements in breathless silence. Nicholas stands with upraised hands, gives a signal—the army forms into a solid body—starts—moves—and in a moment, despite opposition, protestations, pleas and sobs, twenty thousand children have commenced their march to Palestine. On they move, banners flying, songs and cheers floating on the clear air, and while there is many a dimmed eye and choked voice among those gathered to see them start, in the ranks of the Crusaders there is only enthusiasm and joy. On to victory! is their cry as they disappear behind the hills, a winding ribbon of humanity, and soon the sound of their cheers and shouts sinks into silence.

And now let us follow them, as along the Rhine they journey. Across the fields—beyond the river—southward through wilderness and vineyard, they go—marching by an occasional castle rising from some lofty crag, connected in many a childish mind with oft-heard legend and with song.

As they march on, they while away the tedious hours with hymns and tales, the children from the castles telling of knightly deeds done by men of famous name, the peasants, telling of miraculous visions of the Saints; and in the hearing and the telling of the tales, the children became as one family, bound up in one holy purpose—to outdo all deeds of heroic valour which had ever been the theme of song or story.

A motley army they—strangest of all the armies ever seen before—with face and form and voice of youth, but filled with older purpose and courage, as on and on they march with Nicholas in command, the lines stretching behind for several miles; and still are their banners proudly borne aloft, and still as they march, this famous old Crusader's hymn rises on the still air:

> Fairest Lord Jesus,
> Ruler of all Nature,
> O thou of God and man the Son!
> Thee will I cherish,
> Thee will I honour,
> Thou, my soul's glory, joy and crown.
>
> Fair are the meadows,
> Fairer still the woodlands,
> Robed in the blooming garb of spring;
> Jesus is fairer,
> Jesus is purer,
> Who makes the woeful heart to sing.

And still they journey southward, with Palestine their goal, and in their young minds there is no fear of a way to cross the Mediterranean sea, for had not Christ assured Stephen, and a vision revealed to Nicholas, that the drought at that time parching the land was God's evidence that they were to pass through the sea as on dry land, its waters having been parted for their benefit?

So fearlessly and happily they travelled on. through

STEPHEN AND NICHOLAS

the lands of the lords and nobles who owed allegiance to France, and everywhere their fame had preceded them, and in every village they won fresh recruits, until at length their number was so great that no city on the way could contain their army.

Some slept in houses, invited by the kind-hearted, others lay in the streets or market-place, while others lay down outside the walls of the cities, or if they were in open country when night fell, slept in barns or hovels, or by brooks, or under protecting trees, and so weary were they from their tiresome march that wherever they were, it mattered not, they slept as soundly as on beds of down. Then when morning came they ate whatever they had left, or begged or bought what food they could, for some among them still had money in their pockets. The line of march was again formed, the banners unfurled, the crosses uplifted, and with songs and shouts another day was begun. At noon they rested by some stream or in a shaded nook to eat their scanty meal, and then again marched on, feeling more keenly each day the distance lying between them and the land of their dreams, for the great trials of the young Crusaders had begun. Every day the march grew harder and more tiresome to the weary travellers, each meal the supply of food was more scanty, and even those children who had any money were robbed or cheated of it by hangers-on and thieves. Disorder and lawlessness increased rapidly in the ranks of the army, until at last they moved on without any rank or discipline, and under various leaders, who now openly defied the authority of Nicholas. At last they reached the territory now called Switzerland, which was then a number of small districts, mostly belonging to the Emperor; and the army winding through its beautiful valleys and passing along the banks of its turbulent rivers, came at last to the shores of Lake Leman and camped by the walls of Geneva. From thence their task was to cross the trackless heights of the Alps.

Weary and worn, but singing as they went, they journeyed bravely on over Mt. Cenis, which in the Middle Ages was the most frequented of all the mountain passes to Italy, and on that journey many children gave way to exhaustion. The rocks cut their unprotected feet, the air of dark chasms chilled them, they saw no prospect of rest or food until the pass was traversed, and go any farther in such misery they could not. Many turned back, and sadder and wiser, sought again the protection and comfort of their homes.

But the majority of the army still feverishly excited and inflamed with hope, pressed on and on, then suddenly in a moment of unexpected vision, before them in the distance they saw winding rivers, tapestried hills, and vineyards and valleys of such luxuriant beauty as they had never seen in their Northern lands.

With new courage and strength they hurried on now, and soon they were in Italy, where, alas, poor children, they met with all sorts of oppression and cruelty as they journeyed, for the Italians were embittered against the Germans because of the constant wars carried on by their emperors, and visited the sins of their fathers upon these innocent children who were in their power, refusing them entrance to many towns, and subjecting them to all sorts of cruelties. But still such of the army as remained pressed on and on, and then one day, oh, joyous sight, not far beyond they saw the sea, blue and boundless, and on its shore, bathed in sunlight, lay "Genoa, the proud," a vision of fairyland to their dazzled eyes.

Discords were forgotten, songs not sung before for many a tearful day, rose again on the clear air. Crosses

STEPHEN AND NICHOLAS

and banners were again uplifted as of old, and Nicholas was once more prophet and leader, as, forgetful of the past and its miseries, the army of children stood on the 25th day of August, at the gates of the city of Genoa, waiting to be admitted.

Bright were the floating banners, proud were the waiting youths, as Nicholas made his plea:—

"In the name of Christ and his Holy Cross, admit us, his soldiers to your city! Grant us rest on our journey, to rescue the Holy Sepulchre from the hands of the enemy! Men of Genoa, we ask not for transportation across the sea rolling between us and our goal. On the morrow God will part that sea that we may go over as on dry land, to achieve a victory denied to the wise and powerful of the land. Yea, he has said, 'Out of the mouths of babes and sucklings hast thou ordained strength, because of thine enemies, that thou mightest still the enemy and the avenger.' Men of Genoa, open thy gates to us, in the name of Christ!"

A large number of dignified Senators, or rulers of the city, heard the petition of Nicholas, heard it with pity mingled with amusement, and offered the protection of the city for a week to the deluded youths, for by that time—so thought the Senators—the youths would discover their deception and return homeward.

Eagerly did Nicholas and his army accept permission to enter the city whose streets and palaces were in such sharp contrast to those of their own homelands, Genoa being at that time at the height of her prosperity and greatness, but their joyful wonder found its match in that of the inhabitants, whose astonished eyes saw so many fair-haired children marching through their city, with banners and crosses carried high, singing their splendid songs, and full of such grim determination to rescue the Holy Land, a feat which experienced warriors had failed to accomplish.

As the children marched through Genoa, changed indeed was the appearance of their army; of the twenty thousand who had left the banks of the Rhine under the leadership of Nicholas, there were only seven thousand remaining now. Of the rest some were on their homeward journey, some in new homes which they had found by the way, others were lying in undiscovered graves in forest or on hillsides. Only the strongest and most resolute of that great army remained, and in consequence it was the flower of the youth of the Rhinelands, who entered Genoa, rugged and healthy, though their clothes were worn and faded, their feet bruised and bleeding, their faces burned by sun and wind, and their expressions aged and saddened by experience.

The merchants left their desks, the children stopped their play, and stared in wonderment, the grave nobles were move to surprise, and the mothers wiped their eyes as the army of blue-eyed youths marched by.

No sooner had the Senators extended the hospitality of the city to the youths than they decided to retract it, for three reasons: They were afraid of the effect on the morals of the city, which might be produced by the entrance of seven thousand unrestrained boys—also they feared that such a sudden addition to the population might produce a famine, for situated as Genoa was, there was never any too great a quantity of food. Also, most weighty reason of all, the German Emperor was at war with the Pope and in the contest, Genoa was on the Guelph, or papal side. To shelter German children then, even though on a Crusade, would be to harbour foes and to care for a hated race which the Pope had declared outlawed.

In consequence of these reasons the children were told

that they could stay only one night in the city, after all, except those who desired to make it their permanent home, and abandoning their wild scheme, promise to become good citizens.

But the youths laughed scornfully in answer—saying:

"We only *ask* to rest one night. To-morrow you shall see how God cares for his army! Who would remain here, when there lies a path in the sea, between emerald walls, to the land where glory waits us?"

So saying they slept that night, in proud and peaceful hope of the morning's glory, and in the morning rushed early to the shore, that they might see the path across which they were to journey to the promised land. Alas for hopes and promises and visions! The blue waves rippled— the sea rolled on. Hours wore away and yet no path was cleared through the depths, night all too soon came on, and there was no alternative for the army but to leave the city, and then decide upon their next step. Some of the children awoke to the deception of that undivided sea and resolved to stay in Genoa under the conditions imposed by the Senators, for the comforts of the city appealed strongly to them after such hardships as they had experienced.

But on that day, Sunday, August 26th, the remainder of the army which had so proudly and happily entered the city on the day before, went from its gates with hanging heads and sad hearts—a crestfallen band. Outside the city walls they gathered in a field near by, to discuss their plans for the future. Was it wiser to stay and perhaps die in sunny Italy, than to lose their lives on the weary journey separating them from their homes?

One cheery lad made answer, "Are there no other cities which will give us shelter? Why think that Genoa was meant to be the place at which the way through the sea was to be made? Let us push on to the southward until we find the passage which God has promised!"

His courage was contagious, as courage always is, and the diminished band decided to press on still further, until God should show his sign. This resolve made, all turned to Nicholas for his approval of their decision, and so intense had been their excitement during the discussion of their plans that no one had noticed that their leader was no longer one of the group. Alas, for his consecration to a sacred calling, Nicholas was not to be found, either then or later! Their leader, who had led them on to glory, where was he? No one ever knew. Never again was Nicholas seen by any one of those comrades who had followed him so far and so faithfully, trusted him so fully, and barest surmise fills in the mystery of his disappearance.

Nicholas was no high-strung, emotional boy, carried away, as was Stephen, by the glory of his holy calling, he was a calm quiet lad, who, once impressed with the fact that there was work for him to do, always did it to the best of his ability, but always with a keen businesslike instinct of serving his own interests to the best advantage. His father had impressed upon him the glory and rewards which would come to him as leader of a victorious Crusade, and Nicholas had responded to the call.

Now defeat had come instead, and he, the leader of the army, must bear the brunt of the disgrace which would weigh heavily upon his shoulders as long as his life lasted, —of that he felt sure. His comrades were as competent to press on, or to journey homeward without him as under his leadership. So he argued with himself and even as he argued, yielded to a great temptation, and like Esau, sold his honour for a mess of pottage

STEPHEN AND NICHOLAS

A nobleman of Genoa, who was rich and powerful, and who saw in the lad a resemblance to his long lost son sought Nicholas secretly, and offered tempting prospects of a home and such advantages as the lad had never dreamed of having in all his simple life, if he would abandon his leadership and forsake his army, and Nicholas yielded to temptation. With careful strategy he slid away from that little group of disheartened followers, feverishly discussing what was best to do, and all that flock who had trusted him so fully, mourned for him, and mourning, trusted still, accounting him as one whom the Lord God of Hosts had for some wise reason taken from them.

And even while they were mourning for him as for one dead, Nicholas in new garments, more rich and showy than any he had ever worn before, was being shown the wonders of his new home, where servants stood ready to do his bidding, where every article of furnishing was a miracle of fairy fashioning, where cultured voices spoke in gentle tones, and where, oh, rapture far beyond all else, in the near-by stable there stood a prancing steed that was to be his own. Truly a worthy Crusade leader: he—Nicholas, the German lad!

Without a leader now, and without discipline or regulations, the discouraged, disorganised band whom he had deserted, bravely started on again, and reached Pisa, where they had far kinder treatment than in Genoa, and from which place two shiploads of them sailed for the Holy Land, but which we have no record that they ever reached. Those who did not embark, broke up into various small bands and straggling groups, travelling still southward, and at last reached Rome where they told their piteous tale to the authorities. who granted them an audience with the Pope.

TEN BOYS FROM HISTORY

Kneeling before him, they told in graphic worbs the story of their wanderings and sufferings and discouragements, to which unmoved the Pope listened, then, praising their zeal, he commanded them to make no further attempt to reach Palestine, telling them of the hopelessness of the undertaking. But he added, that the cross of a Crusader once assumed, bound one for ever to the Holy Cause, and that when they were older they must fight again for the rescue of the Holy Sepulchre, whenever he should call them to do so.

This bound the children to a repetition of their hardships and adventures, which, considering the courage and suffering of that little band of youths who knelt before him, was little less than cruelty.

Despairing now, and worn out with what they had endured, they were forced to obey the Pope's decree, and so with shattered hopes and dreams of glory for ever abandoned, they retraced their steps, and found their pathway homeward far more trying than the rest of their journey had been.

Many of them died on the way, and of those who lived, it was said in towns and cities through which they passed, that where in departing they passed in parties and troops, happy and never without the song of cheer, they now returned in silence, barefoot and hungry, and with no band of followers.

Day by day they straggled into Cologne—victims of a sad delusion. Alas, how bitterly they had paid for their wilful disobedience!

When asked where they had been, they said they did not know, and had only wild confused tales to tell of strange lands and countries, costumes and customs, and many a mother's heart was broken with sorrow that her boy had not survived the journeying.

STEPHEN AND NICHOLAS

Winter had passed and Spring had come and gone before all the wanderers had returned, all the lost been given up, and for many a year to come, peasants and nobles, with tear-dimmed eyes told the story of the German children's march to the sea, and of the supposed martyrdom of their lost leader, Nicholas—whose father, the afflicted parents whose homes had been desolated by the Crusade, turned on in such a frenzy of bitterness and anger, feeling that he had strongly influenced his son to leadership that they laid violent hands on him and hanged him in revenge.

Meanwhile, during all the weeks while Nicholas and his army were marching southward on their way to Italy, Stephen was still preaching at St. Denys, and his young lieutenants were still gathering recruits for his army from all parts of France—but at length in late June, all was ready except the last preparations for departure, and Stephen then sent out a command to his forces to gather at Vendome, a city near Cloyes, which was not only one of considerable importance, but from which roads lay in many directions from which bands could arrive.

From that moment every day some new band came into Vendome with a young leader in command, and was loudly welcomed by the other waiting bands; while coming across the plains, other groups could be seen marching towards the city, with their flags and oriflammes waving high, and their crosses held higher yet. As they drew near the city their songs could be heard louder and louder until when they reached the city gates, the words were so distinct that their dialect disclosed the province from which they had come.

From every province in France they came, bringing with them their different languages, costumes and peculiarities, and consequently, there was great confusion and variety in the ranks of Stephen's army, but though their dialects and costumes varied greatly, the youths were bound together by a single hope, led by a common aim, as they marched into Vendome ready to start on their perilous journey.

Like the German youths, they were assured that no vessels would be needed to take them across the Mediterranean, for had not Stephen said:

"Between waters which are to be to us as a wall on the right hand and the left, are we to cross the untrodden bed of the sea and with dry feet will we stand on the distant beach by the walls of Acre or of Tripoli. We bear no weapons and we wear no armour! The pathway of other Crusaders may be marked by the stain of blood and the glitter of steel, but our pilgrims' robes are our armour, our crosses are our swords and our hymns shall time our march!"

Not all wore the Crusader's grey coat, but all wore the Cross which was made of muslin cloth and sewed on the right shoulder of the coat. To place the cross there was the duty of the prophets—as the young leaders of each band were called. Receiving the cross was the formal act of enlistment, and proud indeed were the lads who wore them.

At last the latest band had come to Vendome, and fully thirty thousand children were gathered together there, eagerly awaiting the command to start on their journey. What a sight that was, the army of children as they stood waiting for the command to march!

Pleading parents and weeping friends begged the youths to repent and stay at home where their duty lay, but pleas and cries were all counteracted by applause and encouragement from thoughtless enthusiasts, and after religious exercises in which God's blessing was asked, and the oriflammes and crosses raised triumphantly, the army

STEPHEN AND NICHOLAS

formed in line of march, and then with a volume of cheers which drowned the sound of sobs and protests, moved on, out of Vendome under the protection and leadership of Stephen.

It was only a few weeks since the young prophet had been the humble shepherd lad of Cloyes, but that was forgotten now, and as he led his army from Vendome he had assumed a pomp and dignity quite out of harmony with the appearance of his army. A leader of such a mighty host must not walk, so Stephen rode. The Lord's own general and prophet must assume the style which became his rank. He therefore rode in a chariot as splendid as could be procured, covered with rare carpets of brilliant colours. Over his head to protect him from the heat of the sun was a canopy from which there hung draperies of every hue. Around this chariot to guard him and carry out his commands, as well as to add to the impressiveness of his station, rode a band of chosen youths of noble birth, on chargers, dressed in splendid uniforms and armed with lances and spears. This pomp and splendour increased the confidence of his followers, who, too young to see the inconsistency of his conduct, listened to his words as to those of God, and regarded his wishes as law.

Out of Vendome, amid songs and shouts and tears and applause of the crowd gathered to see the departure, moved the ranks of youths, their eyes dazzled with the wonder and the glory of the leader—their hearts on fire to do his bidding. And in Stephen there burned the zeal of the real leader. In order to keep up the spirit of the host, which fatigue would tend to lessen, he spoke to them often in stirring words. At morning or noon or evening when they halted or encamped and also while they marched, he leaned often from his chariot and spoke encouraging words.

TEN BOYS FROM HISTORY

Sometimes they thronged around him so closely wnen he spoke that it was hard work for his guards to protect him from the consequences of their weak homage and as they pushed forward to be near him, many of the weak and small were crushed to death. The veneration for the Boy Prophet was carried to such an extent that all vied with each other to procure a thread of his clothing, a piece of the trappings of his car, while they who had a single hair of his head felt they had a priceless treasure. It is small wonder that this shepherd boy, sensitive as he was to impressions, and duped as he was in the belief that he was anointed by God to a holy calling, and then worshipped by an ever-increasing tide of followers, should have been affected by the rapid change in his circumstances and surroundings. He was evidently possessed of no slight ability to carry out plans, and had much power over people, and his whole nature was aflame with the emotional credulous piety of the Middle Ages. Such was the lad Stephen, shepherd of Cloyes, prophet of the Children's Crusade, when with pomp and ceremony he led his army out of Vendome.

The pathway of his army was marked by far fewer hardships than those the German children were encountering, for the country through which they travelled was more peopled and the distance they had to go much shorter. They did not have to sleep on rocky heights or on freezing moors, and in the lands through which they passed they encountered only sympathy and interest. So their ranks were scarcely thinned by desertion or death, and yet even so, the trip was none too easy, especially on account of the great heat and drought of the summer, to which Stephen constantly referred as a sure sign from God that the sea was to be dried up for their benefit as he had predicted.

His army did not bear heat, want and exhaustion as

STEPHEN AND NICHOLAS

well as the sturdier German children did, and in an incredibly short time its ranks lost all discipline and authority, and at last each one of his band of followers became keen only to outwit the others in a search for food, and in endeavours to hide it, they struggled on—a loose, undisciplined mass, until finally Stephen's authority was entirely lost and the march became only a race for the sea. All original enthusiasm of the army had vanished, and the courage which for a while had been kept up by Stephen's zeal, and by spirited songs and stories, died away, and Stephen was obliged to make use of constant deceptions in answer to questions as to when the weary march would be over, saying that a few more days or hours would bring them to the sea, and so ignorant of geography were the youths that the falsehoods were not detected. Day by day they awoke with fresh hope which was fed by the sight of a castle or walled town which they thought might be Jerusalem, and night after night they lay down victims of a cruel deception—poor deluded, wilful, little pilgrims! On and on they marched through central France, through Burgundy, and beautiful Provence, and finally from the last range of hills they had to climb, there burst on them a view of the cool, blue sea, and from their ranks there came a mighty cheer! With renewed hope they hurried down to the walls of the city of Marseilles which they saw lying below the hills, an enchanting vision of cool green beauty to their untravelled eyes. Their shouts announced their arrival to the people of the city, who hurried to street corners and to market places, and saw with curious and astonished eyes the strangest of all armies which had ever visited their city before, and young and old listened with wide-eyed astonishment to the tale they told. Three hundred miles they had come, those children, in about a month, and the sea was now to divide that they might pass over in safety to accomplish their holy object!

Unlike the German army, their numbers were scarcely lessened, as many new recruits had joined the ranks and replaced those few who had deserted or fallen by the wayside. So it was not a small and tattered or worn-out band who made their appeal to the Marseillian authorities, but an imposing band of twenty thousand youths, still flushed with health and hope.

Having no political reason to refuse them entrance to the city, and possibly rejoicing to have such an influx of pilgrims, permission to stay was given to the host of youths, who with their leader and the older companions who had followed the army, accepted the hospitality of Marseilles and were housed in various places for the one night which was to be the preface to that miracle which would prove their Divine mission.

After a night of fitful sleep and vivid dreams, Stephen at dawn crept out alone, and hastened to the shore of the sea, where he feasted his hungry eyes on its surging depths, crying, "How long, oh, Lord, how long, before thou wilt show thy power?" For hours he remained there, by the sea, and yet there came no pathway for their pilgrim feet to tread. Soon his army had clustered around him, and there they watched, and waited, asking eager questions, and Stephen's hour for victory or defeat had come.

Standing on a rocky height, he spoke, with flashing eyes and ringing voice, yes, and with an honest conviction of the truth of what he said, spoke words of hope and cheer that allowed of no backsliding or complaint, among his followers; and still the weary band kept up their watch by the shore of that surging sea. The afternoon light deepened, the sunset came, night spread its glamour over the scene, and yet the waves rolled on, showing no sign of marvel or of miracle. Over-strained and broken by discouragement, yet still hopeful, the army waited through three long days and nights, and still the sea surged on unchanged, undivided!

Stephen's followers knew the truth at last,—they had been deceived by a false hope, led by a false leader. Crying out against him who had brought them to such a plight, so far from home, they vanished one by one, until of the army that had entered the city, only five thousand remained.

Bewildered, discouraged, frightened, Stephen knew not where to turn for help. Dropping on his knees he prayed earnestly for a voice to tell him of his duty and of God's desire.

Then suddenly his disheartened band of followers saw an unexpected sight. Stephen, the Prophet, marching alone through the streets of Marseilles, waving the Oriflamme, singing a song of triumph, shouting in clear and ringing tones, "God wills it—God wills it!"

They surrounded him, when at last he halted, and he spoke first in denunciation of their unbelief, and then he told of two Marseillian merchants who had come to him even as he was on his knees praying for guidance, and offered him vessels to carry his army to Palestine.

These merchants said they asked no passage money of Christ's soldiers for the trip, the only reward they wished was the consciousness of duty done to pilgrims in a holy cause, the prayers of the children, and the honour of having helped the young Crusaders.

Great was the rejoicing now, and great the shame at having for one moment doubted God's help and the good faith of his servant, Stephen.

Pressing around him as he told his thrilling tale, his

followers begged forgiveness for their lack of faith, which Stephen graciously accorded and became once again the beloved leader, the honoured prophet.

Such vessels as were needed for the expedition were speedily made ready, and in Marseilles loud praises were heard on every side of the generous men who were helping the young Crusaders to fulfil their mission, then people began to gather to watch the little host embark.

It was a thrilling sight—there in that quiet bay, to see the Crusaders, trembling with excitement at this new experience—enter the vessels which were waiting to receive them, while on shore the citizens of Marseilles were crowding to the front to see the expedition start, and the gay colours of the flying banners, the bright costumes of the women, blended with the sunlight in which the fronts of the quaint old houses were bathed, together with the blue water and the bluer sky, made a picture both dazzling and beautiful.

When the little army had entered the ships provided for their use, the solemn ceremonies took place which in those days, when sea voyages were so perilous, always preceded such an expedition. Then, the religious exercises being over, all parts of the ships were examined to see that they were in proper order for such a dangerous voyage, the sailors were stationed at their respective posts, the anchor chains were loosened, ready to release the vessels, and the ropes held in hand. There was a brief silence, then upon the elevated "castle" or stern of each ship, the young army of Crusaders commenced to chant that dear old hymn "Veni Creator Spiritus" which the church in all ages has used on solemn occasions, and as its words floated from one vessel, they were taken up on another until the air was full of harmony which was wafted back to the hills and shore, where the seven vessels were being eagerly

STEPHEN AND NICHOLAS

watched out of sight. With none of the noise of modern steamers, those seven vessels glided out of the quiet harbour, in stately procession and passed beneath the lofty rock of Notre Dame, and the little voyagers were at sea.

Soon their songs grow faint as they float over the water, then die away. After that the flags and banners still tell of joy and hope, until they too are invisible. The day draws to a close, darkness drops down and envelops the seven ships sailing towards the promised land with five thousand courageous little pilgrims on board.

But, alas, for hopes and plans, alas, for the holy ideals of that little band. Not one of them ever realised his ambition!

Two of those ships which sailed so gaily from the harbour of Marseilles, laden with the fair and hopeful youths of France, whose mission was to rescue the Holy Tomb from infidel hands, were wrecked in a wild storm off the Hermit's rock, lying beneath the cliffs of San Pietro.

There beneath the "unplumbed, salt estranging sea" lies Stephen, the boy Prophet—who even while the tempest was hurling his army to death on the open sea, proved the sincerity of his piety; for clinging to a spar, while drifting to a certain doom, he led his little flock in song and prayer, and even as wave after wave dashed over the deck, above the roar of the tempest could his clear triumphant young voice be heard—" In the name of Christ and His cross, be brave. We go to victory—to victory!"

Hideous indeed were the sufferings of the brave youths in the other ships, when they saw their comrades drifting to their death, and little did they dream that they had escaped that terrible storm only to meet still greater perils. Soon they found that they were victims of an infamous treachery, that the merchants who had been so praised in preparing vessels for their use, were simply slave-dealers who had contracted (and probably for an enormous amount of money)—to sell those unsuspecting children to the Mohammedans—the very nation whom the youthful Crusaders had gone forth to conquer, to whom such a consignment of fair young slaves would be of rare value.

Surrounded by vessels of the enemy, they were taken from the ships in which they embarked, and despite their agony of fright and pleading, were carried either to Brijeiah or to Alexandria by their captors, where among the fairest scenes, and the most wonderful and tropical beauty they had ever dreamed of, they were sold into hopeless slavery. Not one of all that army of Stephen's ever saw Europe again, and the Children's Crusade ended as all enterprises end, whether undertaken by young or old, layman or priest, warrior or statesman, when conceived and carried out in a spirit of rebellion and frenzy.

Nicholas and Stephen—boy leaders of the Children's Crusade, one of the most pathetic and thrilling events in all history, one lived—one died. Which, think you, had the right to wear the emblem of the Holy Cross?

PETER OF HAARLEM:
The Boy Who Saved His Country

PETER OF HAARLEM:
The Boy Who Saved His Country

IT was an April day, and Haarlem, an old Dutch town near Amsterdam was gay with tulips, for there in Haarlem are grown the most famous tulips in all the world, as well as hyacinths, and if you had driven through the country roads on that April day, you would have seen the meadows and roadsides overspread with a brilliant carpet of the vari-coloured flowers, while the air was full of the sweet perfume of the hyacinths, and you could have carried away with you as many flowers as you had time and patience to pick.

Holland and its provinces and towns are famous for many other things, as well as for tulips and hyacinths, for it is a country quite different from the others which we visit and study about more often, and although it is a small country in comparison to others which are so vast in territory, yet there has been none more celebrated for courage than brave little Holland, and its fight for independence has made it famous in the historical annals of the world. Sturdy and plucky are the Dutch, and quaint and curious are the customs and manners still prevailing in many of the country districts. Every district has its own costume peculiar to its inhabitants, and the many colours of these costumes, the curious caps worn with them, the heavy wooden shoes, or sabots, which all true Dutch people wear, and the clothes worn by the men, so different from the conventional

TEN BOYS FROM HISTORY

dress of men of other nations, make a picturesque and interesting sight when the Dutch people are gathered together on the day of a " Pardon " or religious fête day.

Their homes, too, are quaint and strange in appearance to our conventional eyes, and it has been said that the Dutch people dressed up like quaint dolls, with their gay little homes and their little canals, which cut up their bright green fields into many sections, live in a country which is like a charming, attractive toy, it is so clean, so tidy and so bright, and it seems a natural thing that the gorgeous tulip should be their favourite flower. And that brings us back to the old town of Haarlem in whose roads we were wandering on an April day.

Now one of the greatest differences between Holland and other countries, is that it lies below the level of the sea, and so has to be very carefully guarded from the surging flood at its very door, or it would be either swept bare by the relentless sea, or entirely wiped out of existence. To prevent this calamity the patient Dutchmen have built wonderful dykes which guard their little country and keep the tyrant sea in check. These dykes are huge banks of earth which tower high above the lowlands and are the only safeguards of the country. Of course, these dykes could only be made gradually, as the sea was turned from one spot to another by dams and locks, and no greater proof of Dutch industry and patience is shown than the way they have protected their land from the sea.

When a dyke has been built, then on the edge of it, a windmill is erected, which works a pump, and as the windmill draws up the water from the sea, it is discharged into a canal. These canals which flow through all Holland in a network of winding ways, run to the sea, and where they meet the sea, in the dykes, great oaken gates, called sluices

PETER OF HAARLEM

are placed across the entrance to the canals, to regulate the amount of water which shall flow into the canals, from the sea. These gates are in charge of men called *sluicers* whose duty it is, when water is needed, to open the gates more or less, according to the amount of water required, and then to close them carefully at night, so that too much water may not flow into the canals, overflow them, and flood the whole country. Even the smallest child in Holland is brought up with a keen knowledge of the grave importance of a sluicer's duty and of the danger to the country if he should neglect it, and the men chosen for that position are always those whose reputation for faithful service is unchallenged.

Naturally, a country lying as Holland lies is very damp and misty, and its entire surface is covered with the network of canals running through the meadows to the sea. If you could stand on a hill and look down on it, it would look like an enormous puzzle, consisting of hundreds of small vivid green pieces cut apart by the canals and decorated by the quaint red-roofed houses of which we have spoken.

Through all the canals flows the same water, and all of them are connected with each other, and are so very wide in some places that there is much traffic on them. Then, too, through miles of the green fields flow the narrower canals, draining the pasturelands, and everywhere one feels the nearness and the menace of the everlasting sea, and the protection of the dykes rearing the huge bulwarks between the peaceful country and its treacherous enemy.

And that brings us back again to Haarlem on that April day when the quaint little town was gay with the red and yellow tulips and the air sweet with the scent of hyacinths.

On that bright spring day a little boy whose name is

said to have been Peter, and whose father was a sluicer, had for his dinner some cakes of which he was very fond, and which his mother had baked because she knew how much Peter liked them.

Peter was a very unselfish boy, and whenever he had anything he liked, his first thought always was to share it with someone else. So, as soon as he had finished his meal, he jumped up from the table and begged his mother to let him go to see a poor blind man who lived not far away, and to let him carry with him those cakes which had not been eaten.

His mother was pleased with this thought of Peter's for the poor old man, and at once brought a basket and filled it with cakes for him to carry to the invalid, while Peter's father was making him promise not to stay out too late, and soon the boy was on his way to his friends, happy in the beauty of the day, and in the thought of the pleasure his present would give the blind man.

And he was not mistaken, the old man was delighted with the cakes, and at once broke and ate one, while he began to tell Peter one of the stories for which he was famous, and which he knew Peter loved to hear. But Peter suddenly remembered his promise not to stay out late, and finally became so uneasy that he told the old man he must not wait to hear the end of the story, and, hastily bidding him farewell, started towards home.

His path lay beside the dyke, and along its grassy banks grew beautiful wild flowers of many varieties, so numerous and attractive that Peter decided to pick a bunch of them to carry home to his mother, who was so much of an invalid that she was seldom out of the house. So he picked a few here and a few there—blue and yellow and pink, until he had a handful of those varieties of which he knew his

PETER OF HAARLEM

mother was most fond, and as he walked on, to keep himself from feeling lonesome, he hummed a gay little song.

Presently, he stopped, and neither sang nor smiled, as he looked at a slender thread of water trickling through the grass. Where did it come from? Surely not from the canal, and there was nowhere else for it to come from unless it came from the dyke itself.

The thought was enough to make even a child turn pale and tremble. Only the dykes stood between the boundless sea and the safety of little Holland. He looked again, and to his imagination, the stream seemed greater already. What could he do? Night was coming on, the road was a solitary one. There was only the barest chance of anyone passing that way whom he might hail, or of whom he could ask advice.

Then came a quick recollection of his promise to his father, and he started homeward again, but a force as mighty as a giant's grasp, made him turn back again to watch that trickling stream of water.

He was near one of the great oaken sluices, and bounding up beside it he carefully examined the dyke. There, as small as his finger, was a hole—strange and unaccountable happening,—and through that little hole was flowing the stream of water at his feet.

Like lightning the flash of intuition came to Peter, if that hole were not stopped up instantly, the force of the flow through it would rapidly increase from the pounding of that mighty sea behind it. In a night the flood would break through the dyke and perhaps destroy all the homes in Holland.

What could he do? No stone would fit the hole, no amount of earth packed into the crevice could resist the pressure of the water. Peter was desperate. Forgotten now were his bunch of flowers which fell unheeded from his hand. He strained his eyes in a vain search for travellers on that lonely road, vainly he shouted out for help until his throat was hoarse. What could he do? It was no common instinct that came in that lightning flash to Peter. Climbing again up the steep bank, from stone to stone, he thrust his finger in the hole and, oh, joy, it fitted! It stopped the trickling water for the moment, but, oh, what would happen when he took it out?

Ah, it was as clear as daylight, what to do. He would not take it out until someone should come to relieve him. Forgetful of what this idea might bring to him, if carried out, he chuckled with a boyish delight in this real adventure.

"Ha, ha!" he said to himself. "The water *can't* come down now. Haarlem shall not be drowned while I am here to keep the flood back."

For awhile excitement kept him warm and fearless. Then the chill darkness of the night surrounded him. All sorts of strange noises fell upon his unaccustomed ears, he seemed to see giants and demons lurking near, ready to pounce upon him and kill him. Although he was a sturdy lad, tears came at last, when he could no longer keep back thoughts of his comfortable bed at home, of the parents who might be even then worrying about his safety, although as he before remained over night with the old man, Jansen, he felt that his mother and father had probably gone to bed and to sleep, while he was out in the dark night alone and in such a misery of pain. The pain grew greater, the misery harder to bear every moment now, and still Peter kept his finger in that dangerous hole.

He tried to whistle, hoping to attract the attention of some straggling traveller, but his teeth chattered so much

PETER OF HAARLEM

that he gave it up, and then he remembered what he had been taught at his mother's knee, and Peter prayed to the great God who could control the surging sea and protect a boy who was doing his best. Peter was only a child, but if he ever prayed with his whole heart, he prayed so that night in the darkness, with his numbed finger thrust through that hole in the dyke, and when his prayer was said he somehow felt braver, stronger and older than before, and in his heart he said:

"I will not take it out till someone comes. I will stay till morning."

Longer and longer grew the hours, the minutes, the seconds, and yet he never moved—there were strange noises in his head, his thoughts were confused, pictures of his playmates, of events long ago forgotten danced before his eyes. He was not sure he could draw his finger out of the hole even if he wished to do so, it felt so strangely numb. What did it mean that knives seemed to be cutting, and pins pricking him from head to foot? What would happen if no one ever found him—no one ever came to help?

At last the rose and silver of the dawn flushed the sky. Day had come and along that lonesome road came the first traveller in all the hours of Peter's vigil.

A clergyman whose night had been spent by the bedside of a sick parishioner, hurrying homeward on the path beside the dyke, heard a groan, a feeble sound of one in mortal agony. Turning, he glanced, first here and there, and looking up, at last, he saw beside the dyke, the figure of a child writhing in agony.

In a single bound, the clergyman stood beside him exclaiming:

"In the name of wonder, boy, what are you doing here?"

TEN BOYS FROM HISTORY

"I am keeping the water from running out," said Peter. "Oh, can't you ask them to come *quick.*"

And they did. The town of Haarlem, even Holland itself, had been saved, through the courage of a little boy who did his duty, and from that day to this there has never been a child in Holland who has not heard the stirring story of Peter, whose pluck was worthy of a sluicer's son, and whose name will never be forgotten, or effaced from the page of historic legend.

DAVID: THE SHEPHERD BOY

David and Goliath

DAVID: THE SHEPHERD BOY

A RARE good fortune it is to have a friend so true and so faithful that it is as safe to tell him a secret as to whisper it to yourself, one to whom your interests are as important as his own, and who would do any sort of unselfish act to show his devotion to you. It was just such a comradeship as this which existed between two boys of long ago, the story of whose intimacy has come down to us from Bible times as a most wonderful example of what a friendship can be.

Those boys were David, the son of Jesse of Bethlehem, and Jonathan, the son of Saul, King of Israel, and when you hear two persons spoken of as "a David and a Jonathan" you may know that they are the closest kind of friends.

To appreciate thoroughly the friendship between David and Jonathan, and what it meant to both of them, let us go back a little into the history of the time in which the boys lived, and look at the circumstances which led up to their friendship, for that is very important to a clear understanding of the story of David and Jonathan.

At that time the kingdom of Israel was in a deplorable condition, for the Philistines, a war-like tribe who lived in a small territory on the coast, had over-run and conquered most of Israel, and Samuel who was the aged guide and advisor of the Israelites, as well as the last of the judges and the first of the prophets of Israel, saw that the only hope for his people lay in having a higher moral standard and a central government. To bring this about, Samuel established the schools of the prophets in Ramah and other cities, where men could be trained to teach their nation how to live wiser, purer lives—and Samuel also anointed Saul as King of Israel, and for a while Saul ruled wisely and well. Then he disobeyed the command of God, and began to care for conquest in war only when it brought him glory or the spoils of battles, and Samuel seeing this, was much troubled, and finally went to Saul and told him that he must repent and do differently or he would no longer be worthy to be the King of Israel, that God demanded more honest service than he was giving. Saul was considerably troubled at this plain speaking of Samuel and promised to do better in future, but when Samuel left him, it was with a heavy heart, for he felt sure that there would be need of a new king—that Saul would not keep his promises.

And so Samuel at once began to look for a man whom he could anoint as the future King, although no one knew of this purpose but himself, and the voice of God within him inspired him to go to Bethlehem and seek among the sons of Jesse for the King he wished to find. So Samuel went to Bethlehem, but in order that the real purpose of his visit might not be discovered, he took with him beside the horn of oil with which he would anoint the new King if he should find him, also a young calf to offer as a sacrifice, that he might have a suitable excuse to give to the people for his visit.

Of course the coming of Samuel created a great excitement in the little town of Bethlehem, for the people feared that he came to reprove them for some wrong-doing, until Samuel assured them that this was not so, that he came peaceably, and in proof of it invited them to the sacrifice

DAVID THE SHEPHERD BOY

which he was preparing to offer on a hill just outside the gate of the city. According to the rule of Oriental hospitality, it was customary that some prominent man from the village should invite Samuel to return to his home after offering the sacrifice, to break bread with him and to pass the night under his roof if Samuel desired to do so, and as Samuel had invited Jesse to the sacrifice, it came about quite naturally that, as Samuel desired, it was Jesse's home to which the aged Prophet went.

After they had arrived there, Samuel and Jesse sat and talked together alone, for although Jesse had eight sons and two daughters, and they were no longer children, the Eastern custom forbade a man's family to enter his presence unless he expressly asked them to do so. And so Samuel and Jesse were alone together, until Samuel asked Jesse if he had no sons. Jesse replied that he had, and Samuel then requested to see them. It was natural for a father to be pleased at such a request and Jesse at once sent for Eliab, his eldest son, who promptly came into the presence of his father and the aged Prophet, and Samuel looked earnestly at the tall, handsome fellow, but a voice within him told Samuel that Eliab was not the king-to-be, and after a brief talk with the young man, he was dismissed, and Jesse called another and then another of his sons, until Samuel had seen seven of them, but the prophet only shook his head as he saw each one of them, for the voice of inspiration or instinct said within him:

"Neither hath the Lord chosen this." Then Samuel turned once more to Jesse and asked:

"Are here all thy children?" And Jesse answered reluctantly:

"There remaineth yet the youngest, and behold he keepeth the sheep."

TEN BOYS FROM HISTORY

Then Samuel bade Jesse send for David, which he did, and David, who was as usual roaming with his flock in the Judean pasture-land, was greatly surprised to see a messenger coming to him in breathless haste, and still more was he surprised to receive his father's message that he was to come home at once, as the prophet Samuel had asked to see him before leaving. It was an unexpected command, but young David was always ready for any emergency, and so, simply taking up his shepherd's staff, which was a long stick with a handle crooked in such a way that by its aid David could examine the limbs of his flock, or roll a sheep over with it, when unruly and without further preparation, David accompanied the messenger, although filled with wonder as to the reason for being summoned to appear before the aged prophet Samuel.

See him as he enters his home and stands before Samuel, red-cheeked, fair-skinned, glowing with health and happiness, with arms strong enough to break a bow of steel, and with limbs like a deer's in their swiftness to escape a foe or to scale a wall. Sturdy and fearless he stood before Samuel, the picture of youthful vigour and courage, and when Samuel had scarcely more than glanced at him, the voice of God spoke within the prophet saying:

"Arise, anoint him, for this is he."

Then Samuel rose with simple earnestness and laid a hand on David's shoulder, looking long and solemnly into the clear bright eyes which answered his glance, then more solemnly still, Samuel took up the horn of oil which he had brought with him, and with the customary ceremony, anointed David, the fair-haired young shepherd boy, to be the future King of Israel. As only kings were anointed and Samuel always performed this ceremony, Jesse could not have failed to understand the solemn rite, although he must

DAVID THE SHEPHERD BOY

have marvelled over it, wondering why it should be performed over this, his youngest and least important son. Doubtless, although the Bible narrative does not tell us so, the aged prophet later spoke to Jesse of the meaning of his act, and one can imagine Jesse's flutter of heart at the thought that one of his boys should have been chosen to fill such a great position. David also, young as he was, must have understood in some measure what the ceremony meant, although he must have been completely at a loss to understand how he, a mere child, could be the Lord's anointed. Probably, like any other boy of to-day, he wanted to ask questions, but there was not the freedom allowed young people in those days that there is now and David, looking from the awe-struck face of his father, to the solemn one of the prophet, doubtless kept silent. Then with an appropriately reverential farewell to the aged prophet he must have been sent from the presence of Jesse and Samuel, sent back again to his accustomed task and to await the fulfilling of that destiny which, from the moment when he thrilled at the touch of the prophet's hand on his head, and the sound of his solemn words, he felt sure was in some way to link his life in consecrated service to that of the people of Israel.

But that belief did not alter his conduct in his daily routine of duty, and with the faithfulness which was one of his marked characteristics, he continued to care for his sheep, tending them with increased watchfulness under the stimulus of his new day-dream.

And from that moment David had unconsciously taken the motto which was his through all his adventurous life:

"I shall not raise my hand against the Lord's anointed."

TEN BOYS FROM HISTORY

From that hour when he went back to tend his sheep, after Samuel's visit, to the time when his destiny was fulfilled, David, even under the stress of fierce temptation, never moved a finger to hasten events; never tried to force his way to the throne of Israel, but with buoyant courage, did his duty day by day, and the monotony of his early shepherd's life was varied only by an occasional unexpected adventure.

Look—listen—as he wanders over the hillside at dusk, he shows alarm—he hears a dreaded sound! Ah, yes, one he knew too well—the stealthy glide of a creeping foe coming to attack his flock.

Alone, with only his sling for weapon, in that wild unpeopled country, the shepherd boy stands, brave and alert, ready to protect his sheep. Ah, a lion! the stealthy beast creeps nearer, nearer.

Suddenly David draws his sling, the stone strikes the lion between the eyes, he falls by a single shot. But look—this is not the end of the battle. Even while David is encountering the lion, that most dreaded of all foes of the flock, a huge bear glides with stealthy steps, and seizes a lamb. Quick as an arrow David hurls himself upon the monstrous beast, who drops his prey and rises in angry power on his hind legs to hug and crush his enemy. But David is too quick for him, he grasps the bear by the jaw with iron force, grapples with him, the great creature snarls, moans, writhes and is no more, while David, hot with the joy of victory, turns back to quiet his frightened flock.

Does not this encounter give a hint of the fearless courage that made David such a famous warrior in later life?

Now let us note another side of his many-sided character while we listen to the melodies he so dearly loved to

DAVID THE SHEPHERD BOY

play on his harp as he wandered over the hills and plains with his flock. David had in him the making of a mighty warrior, a great king, but he had too, a dreamy, sensitive, poetic side to his nature, which made him deeply appreciate and enjoy all the beauty of nature which he tried to express in his music, and which long years later, came out more clearly in those wonderful psalms which he wrote, and which have comforted and helped so many generations of Christian people.

In those days Saul was becoming less and less of a dignified, self-controlled leader, as he began to realise that he was not powerful enough to hold his people, and he frequently gave way to fits of terrible anger or prolonged melancholy, from which no one could rouse him. At that time when the Philistines were gaining so many victories over the Israelites, it was most important that Saul should not give way to such attacks, as they unfitted him to perform his public or private duties, and every means of quieting him was tried, but in vain. Finally, it was suggested that music has a soothing effect on troubled spirits, and when the idea was mentioned to Saul it pleased him, and he at once commanded that a musician be found and brought to him. Then came the question of who that musician should be, and one of Saul's counsellors said:

"Behold, I have seen a son of Jesse, the Bethlehemite, that is cunning in playing and a comely person, and the Lord is with him."

The description pleased Saul and he at once sent a messenger to Jesse, saying:

"Send me David, thy son, which is with the sheep."

And so once again, there came to David a new experience for which he had had no preparation, and again, as before, he neither refused nor questioned the call to a different life, but while Jesse, his father, was preparing a present to send to Saul by David, according to the custom of the times, David was making hasty preparations to leave home. Soon he was ready to set off, and taking with him an ass laden with bread, a bottle of wine and a young kid, which were Jesse's present to Saul, on he journeyed over the hills and through the valleys until he reached the court of the King, and presently stood in the presence of Saul, who almost as soon as he had looked at the lad with his fair, bright face and sturdy figure, took a great fancy to him, and commanded him to become one of his household and to come and play to him whenever he should be summoned, and also sent this message back to Jesse:

"Let David, I pray thee, stand before me, for he hath found favour in my sight."

So David stayed at the King's court, and whenever Saul gave way to an attack of anger or depression, the young minstrel would hasten to him, and play melodies grave and gay, sweet and brilliant, playing with such skill that before he knew it, Saul would be in good humour again, or drop into a deep, refreshing sleep, and little did he dream that the lad who had such power to soothe and amuse him had been anointed by Samuel to rule over Israel in his place. That David thought often and earnestly about this, would be only natural to suppose, and we can but fancy that in those days amid surroundings such as he had never had before, the young lad learned much of the manners and customs of a king's life, and learned too, from the weakness that he saw in Saul's nature what a king ought to be and do. Probably much of David's tact in dealing with men and circumstances at a later day came from his observations in those early days when he was but a minstrel at the court of Saul.

How long he remained there, we do not know, but

DAVID THE SHEPHERD BOY

until Saul's attacks of passion and melancholy had been entirely overcome. Then, in the same spirit of unquestioning obedience as he showed before to the call of circumstances, as soon as he was no longer needed by Saul, David went back again to his home in Bethlehem and again tended his father's flocks in the Judean pasture-lands.

The Israelites and the Philistines were still at war, and the two armies were now encamped against each other on opposite ridges that overhung a valley, called the valley of the Terebinth, about sixteen miles from Bethlehem.

Battles in those days were sometimes merely encounters between two champions chosen by the opposing armies to fight for them; but the Philistines had given no hint to the Israelites that this was to be their plan of action, when suddenly, out from their camp there burst forth Goliath, the last and mightiest of the giants of Gath, and shouted out a challenge to the Israelites, saying:

"Why are ye come out to set your battles in array? Am not I a Philistine and ye servants to Saul? Choose you a man for you and let him come down to me. If he be able to fight with me and kill me, then will we be your servants, but if I prevail against him, then shall ye be our servants and serve us!" And he added in a mighty voice that rang through the valley:

"I defy the armies of Israel this day! Give me a man that we may fight together!"

Colossal and terrifying, the great monster stood, like a glittering mountain of power as the rays of the sun fell upon him, for he was over ten feet tall, and his coat of mail was as heavy as bags of gold would be, and shone like a mirror, and on his head was a huge helmet of brass, and even his mighty limbs were covered with shining metal. He carried a brass spear with a head heavier than that of ten ordinary spears, and the staff of it was as huge as a young birch tree, while before him walked the bearer of his shield, glittering too in the rays of the sun. A mighty monster, he, Goliath, the giant of Gath, as he faced the army of the Israelites and thundered forth his challenge to them to find a warrior bold enough to fight with him, and the Israelites were filled with fear as they saw him, and Saul's heart was heavy with terror, and he at once offered great riches and the hand of his daughter to any warrior who would accept Goliath's challenge. But for forty days not a man answered the challenge or attempted to win the reward offered by Saul.

Then David, who was still tending his father's flocks, but whose three elder brothers were with the army of the Israelites, was sent by his father to carry supplies of food to them. Of course, David had heard much at home that interested him deeply in the armies and their manœuvres, and now he could scarcely restrain his joy at the thought of seeing the encampments for himself, and he got up early the next morning and leaving his sheep with a keeper, set out gleefully, even though what he had to carry was a heavy burden, for he was taking a large quantity of parched corn and ten loaves of bread to his brothers, as well as ten cheeses to the captain of their division of the army. But he was so happy at the change in his monotonous life that he did not mind the length of the journey nor the weight of his burden.

And when he saw the tents of the encampments lying before him, he thrilled with the courage and the desire of a born warrior, and quickly leaving his provisions with the keeper of supplies, he ran forward to the division of the camp where his brothers were, and eagerly greeted them, but they seemed not at all glad to see him, even though he had come to bring them sorely needed food.

DAVID THE SHEPHERD BOY

Jealousy is one of the worst faults a person can have, and it is to be feared that David's family all felt it and showed it for this youngest brother, who though a mere boy of seventeen, had received honours, and shown ability far beyond their own, instead of rejoicing in his good fortune, as they should have done.

But David was evidently accustomed to their manner, and was unconscious then of everything but his keen desire to know what the plans of the two armies were, and poured out question after question, without heeding the impatience of his brothers' answers.

And as he stood talking, there suddenly stood before him the glittering monster Goliath, and again his challenge rang through the valley; and as always when Goliath was seen or heard, the men of Israel turned away and fled in terror. But not so David. He was thrilled at the sight of the mighty giant and asked the men who stood by him:

"What shall be done to the man that killeth this Philistine and taketh away the reproach of Israel? For who is this Philistine that he should defy the armies of the living God?"

And the men answered him that Saul had promised riches and honour and his daughter's hand in marriage to him who should kill Goliath.

And Eliab, David's oldest brother, listened while David questioned the men, and being very angry at David's presence, said bitterly:

"Why camest thou down hither, and with whom hast thou left those few sheep in the wilderness. I know thy pride and the naughtiness of thy heart, for thou art come down that thou mightest see the battle."

But David, instead of showing anger at such an unkind speech, merely answered:

"What have I *now* done? Is there not a cause," and

TEN BOYS FROM HISTORY

paying no further attention to Eliab, turned away, asking every man he met the same question he had asked before, until finally his persistency attracted so much attention, that Saul was told about this lad who was showing such unusual interest in the rewards to be given for facing Goliath in battle, and Saul at once sent for David, who by this time was flushed with excitement, and with the contagious enthusiasm of the battlefield, and he answered Saul like an old and mighty soldier.

"Let no man's heart fail because of him. Thy servant will go and fight with this Philistine."

Think of it, a slender inexperienced young shepherd lad taking up a challenge like that of Goliath!

Saul was astonished at David's words, and exclaimed, "Thou art not able to go against this Philistine and fight him, for thou art but a youth, and he a man of war from his youth."

Throwing his shoulders back, and standing with head held high and eyes bright with determination, David answered proudly:

"I kept my father's sheep, and there came a lion and a bear and took a lamb out of the flock, and I went out after him, and delivered it out of his mouth, and when he rose against me, I caught him by the beard and smote him and slew him. The Lord that delivered me out of the paw of the lion and the bear, he will deliver me out of the hand of this Philistine."

For a moment Saul looked in silent awe at this brave young warrior—then in a voice trembling with admiration and with emotion, he said with solemn emphasis:

"Go, and the Lord be with thee."

And then roused by the contagion of David's fearless enthusiasm, and by the excitement of trusting a mere boy to

DAVID THE SHEPHERD BOY

give battle to the great Goliath, Saul, with his own hand, dressed David in his own suit of armour for the encounter, giving him his heavy coat of mail, his glittering brass helmet, and even bound his own sword at David's side. At first David's delight was great that he was wearing the armour of a real warrior. But when he tried to walk or run, the heavy coat of mail hindered him and the weight of the sword and helmet made him feel like a captive in chains, and at last he cast them off, saying to Saul:

"I cannot go with these."

And although Saul showed his consternation at this young champion of the Israelites against Goliath, going to battle without armour or sword, he made no attempt to persuade David into doing other than as he desired. And David stood before him again, this time, wearing his simple shepherd's dress, and feeling both free and happy again. Then taking up his staff, he went to a near-by brook and from its bed picked out five smooth white stones,—notice how careful he was to choose smooth stones. These he put in a bag which hung at his side, and then with only his sling in his hand, he advanced towards the giant, who having heard that David had accepted his challenge, had advanced to meet him in all his power and show of glittering armour and weapons.

Now Goliath had not heard of David's youth, and when he saw that his adversary was only a fair strong boy, the giant grew scornful, and seeing David's staff and sling, he shouted contemptuously in a voice that rang from ridge to ridge, across the great valley:

"Am I a *dog* that thou comest to me with stones?" adding:

"Come with me, and I will give thy flesh unto the fowls of the air, and to the beasts of the fields."

But David paid no heed to the scorn, but sturdy and strong he stood and faced Goliath, answering:

"Thou comest to me with a sword and with a spear and with a shield, but *I* come to thee in the name of the Lord of Hosts, the God of the armies of Israel, whom thou hast defied. This day will the Lord deliver thee with my hand and take thine head from thee, and I will give the carcasses of the Philistines this day unto the fowls of the air and the wild beasts of the earth, that all the earth may know that there is a God in Israel, and all this assembly shall know that the Lord saveth not with sword and spear, for the battle is the Lord's and he will give you into our hands."

A pretty long speech and a pretty decided statement to be made by a shepherd-boy—was it not? David's positive assurance that he could kill Goliath, and that God was with the army of Israel, showed the boy to be no ordinary boy, carried away by warlike enthusiasm.

Goliath heard with mighty contempt and anger, the retort of David and his taunt, and advanced in all his power and glory towards him, while David, never taking his eyes off the giant's face, quietly put his hand in his bag, slowly took out one of the stones he had so carefully selected, and slung it with the unerring aim for which he was famous.

With fatal accuracy it struck Goliath between the eyes. The mighty giant groaned, and fell—slain by the hand of David, who, as he had no sword of his own, hastily knelt on Goliath's body, drew his sword from its sheath, and with it cut off the gaint's head, and stripped him of his valuable armour, to carry to Bethlehem as a trophy.

David, so young, so inexperienced in the art of war, had killed the champion of the enemy. It seemed incredible. Through the ranks of both armies the news spread

DAVID THE SHEPHERD BOY

like wildfire, and when the Philistines realised what had happened, they were so terrified for fear of what might follow, that they fled, with the victorious Israelites in hot pursuit, who with cheers and shouts and great slaughter pursued them to the nearest city, and then returned to despoil the tents of the vanquished enemy, singing loud songs of triumph.

And then David, flushed with victory, came before Saul carrying with him the head of the giant. It is easy to picture Saul's absolute astonishment when he realised that the conquering hero of his army was this mere youth, so unlike his other warriors.

But he talked long and eagerly with David, asking all sorts of questions about his manner of slaying Goliath, and while they talked, Jonathan, Saul's son, stood near them, listening and watching, and as he heard David's stirring tale of victory, he was filled with admiration for the boy who had done such a mighty deed; and, in that instant, as the Bible says, "the soul of Jonathan was knit with the soul of David," and the friendship of David and Jonathan was begun. David's eyes flashed back an answering glance of interest to the King's son, and there was a quick response of each to the other. And that being so, you can imagine the joy of both the youths when Saul told David that he was to go no more home to his father's house to tend his flocks, but was to be thereafter his armour-bearer, or the member of his household who came into the closest relation with the king. On hearing this great piece of news, David glanced proudly at Jonathan, and Jonathan at once led David away and took from him his shepherd's dress, and clothed him in his own garments, giving him even his girdle and his sword, which was the greatest honour he could have conferred on David, the sign that he felt David had, by his courageous act, proved himself more worthy to be the heir to a throne, than he, the king's own son, was. And, too, he felt such a thrill of affection for this new friend, David, that he could not help doing something to show it. And then and always, Jonathan's friendship for David was absolutely free from all taint of jealousy, and he always stood aside, that honours might be heaped upon his friend, even those which by the rights of inheritance, should have been his own.

And so David began his new life at the court of Saul, with Jonathan, his new friend, and the first happy days passed only too quickly. David went out wherever Saul sent him, doing the King's bidding so well and so wisely that Saul set him in command over his men of war, who all gladly obeyed David. Although he was so young, he ruled so tactfully that all the people, and even Saul's ministers grew more and more fond of the youth who had killed Goliath, while Jonathan rejoiced in every honour paid to his friend, and had not one bit of envy in his heart, that David was so popular and so powerful. But Saul was less noble in nature than Jonathan his son was, and when one day, not long after David had killed Goliath, the men, women and children from all the cities of Israel, trooped out to meet King Saul, singing and dancing and playing musical instruments in celebration of David's victory, and the women sang—

"Saul hath slain his thousands and David his ten thousands."

This made Saul very angry and very jealous, for it was a revelation of the strength of the national feeling against him, and as he heard the shrill chant, he exclaimed with fierce jealousy:

"They have ascribed unto David his ten thousands and

DAVID THE SHEPHERD BOY

to me they have ascribed but thousands, and what can *he* have more but the kingdom?"

From that moment, Saul was never fond of David, but always bitterly envious of him, and watched to see how and when he could do the lad an injury.

The violence of his rage and jealousy threw him into one of his old paroxysms, and as of old, David was called to soothe him by the music of his harp. But the sight of David threw Saul into a still worse fever of madness, and in anger he hurled his spear, the symbol of his royalty, at David, crying:

"I will smite David even to the wall with it," but David was quick enough to avoid it, and when at another time Saul attempted the same thing, David again slipped aside, and the spear simply struck the wall. This agility of David's made Saul even more angry than before, and increased his fear of the wonderful youth, whom Saul felt had the blessing of God, which had been taken from him. So strong was Saul's dislike of David now, that finally he sent him away from the house, giving him a position where he would have less influence than formerly, for he would be only captain over a thousand men, but the new position only increased David's popularity. He ruled those under him with such wisdom that all the people loved him, and Saul was, of course, more jealous and angry than before, and yet afraid of him too, and he began to think of another way to rid himself of the troublesome rival.

When David had fought Goliath, he was promised the hand of Saul's eldest daughter in marriage, if he should be victorious, which promise had not been kept as yet, and now Saul remembered this, and offered to redeem the promise by giving David his daughter, Merab, as wife, hoping that in this way, he would not only rouse David's gratitude, but make him feel in honour bound to fight the Philistines again, for his wife's sake, and Saul hoped that they might kill him.

Although in our day, David would have been far too young to think of being married, in those days such things were different, and David accepted the hand of Merab, but at the last moment, through some new caprice of Saul's, the promise was broken and Merab became another man's wife. But Saul's younger daughter, Michal, who had admired David's behaviour ever since he had been her father's armour-bearer, was as fond of him as her brother, Jonathan was, and when she told her father this, he was greatly pleased and said to himself that she should marry David, who would then fight the Philistines for her sake and be killed by them. And when David objected to marrying her, saying that it was no easy matter for a poor man to marry the daughter of a king, Saul's messengers answered:

"The King requireth no dowry from him, only that he kill a hundred Philistines."

This pleased David, for he was a born warrior, and he did not know that the King's purpose in this agreement was to have him fall by the sword of the enemy. So even before the marriage took place, he was so eager to fulfil the king's request that he and his men went out and killed twice as many Philistines as Saul demanded, and came home unhurt, and although Saul was angry at this, he was obliged to give him Michal in marriage, but from that moment, Saul hated David more fiercely than ever, and was determined to kill him, especially when he saw that the people loved David more and more deeply for his wisdom and bravery. Intent on this purpose, Saul even called his ministers and servants together and told them that they must kill David, and he told Jonathan this too, and Jonathan, loving David as

DAVID THE SHEPHERD BOY

he did, was filled with fear that his father's wishes would be carried out, and so he hurried to David with the news of his father's command, and begged David to hide until the next day, saying that meanwhile he would go to his father and try to alter his feelings.

When David heard Saul's command, it did not frighten him as much as it did Jonathan, for he was almost fearless by nature, but he listened to Jonathan intently, and promised to do what he asked, and as soon as Jonathan had left him and gone to Saul, David fled to a secret place and hid there, while Jonathan, having sought his father, began to say good things about David, even though he saw there was danger of arousing his father's fierce anger by what he said.

But he spoke boldly, because of his love for David, saying: "Let not the King sin against David, because he hath not sinned against thee, and because his works have been to thee very good. For he did put his life in his hand and slew the Philistines, and the Lord wrought a great salvation for all Israel. Thou sawest it and did rejoice, wherefore then, wilt thou sin against innocent blood, to slay David without a cause."

It was a brave thing for Jonathan to speak so frankly to his father, and he would have been more frightened in doing it, had not his love of David given him courage. And he had his reward, for not only did Saul listen attentively to him, but was touched by his plea, and when he finished speaking, swore solemnly:

"As the Lord liveth, he shall *not* be slain."

Jonathan scarcely waited to hear the words, before he hurried from his father's presence and ran as fast as he could run to David's hiding-place to tell him the good news, that he was not to be killed. And then he insisted

TEN BOYS FROM HISTORY

that David should go back with him to the king's court, which David did, and when Saul saw him, old memories stirred in his heart and he welcomed David affectionately as he had done in times past.

For a while David remained with Saul and Jonathan and as all went on peacefully, he and Jonathan had many happy hours together. Then there was war again with the Philistines, and David was sent out to fight them, and was again victorious over them, slaying them with such a great slaughter that those who remained alive fled from him, in fear and dismay. And although Saul was glad of David's victory over the enemies of Israel, the old jealousy of his young and powerful rival again overcame him and he had or pretended to have one of his old attacks of rage, and as in old times, David was called to soothe his inflamed spirit. But while he was playing, Saul was filled with jealous fury, and again hurled his spear at the young musician, and again David slipped aside and escaped it, and the spear hit the wall instead of his body—then he fled to his own house, more worried than he had ever been before; for now he saw clearly that Saul would never give up his purpose to kill him.

This he told his wife, Michal, who knew her father's cruel, jealous disposition, even better than Saul did, and was much alarmed for her husband's safety.

That night, Saul, following out his determination, to rid himself of David, sent watchers to guard David's house and make sure that he did not escape in the night, and though they did not go into the house to kill him at once, because of an old Oriental superstition that only evil would come to those who entered a home by night, they planned to enter at daybreak and arrest him.

Michal, with a woman's keen instinct, when she saw

the messengers outside, guessed their purpose and at once she said to David:

"If thou save not thy life to-night, to-morrow, thou shalt be slain," and then she told David of her plan to save him, which he thought was a good one. After a hasty farewell, she assisted her husband to escape through a window on the opposite side of the house from where the king's messengers were crouched, and David under cover of the darkness crept stealthily away and escaped once more from Saul's hand. When she had seen him creep away in the darkness, Michal went back into the house and dressing up an image, as if it were a man, she laid it in David's bed, and covered it, head and all, with a long thick coverlet, and at dawn when Saul's messengers forced an entrance, demanding David, Michal answered:

"He is sick."

The men went away and told Saul this, but he did not believe it, and sent them back to bring David to the palace in his bed, if they found him too sick to walk, and it must have been a moment of triumph for Michal, who had worked so hard to save her husband's life, and who knew that he was, even then, far away, when she led Saul's messengers to the bed, where they found, not their victim, but only an image.

When Saul heard of this, his rage was almost beyond bounds, but Michal did not care, for she knew that David was safe now, and her answers to her father's reproaches at her conduct in helping David to escape were as fearless as possible.

All this took time, and meanwhile, David, now an outcast from his home, had hurried to Ramah, a city on a height about three miles west of Gibeah, where he found Samuel at the School of Prophets, and when he told Samuel all that Saul had done to him, Samuel felt sorely against Saul, and went with David to Naioth, hoping that they might in that way escape Saul's messengers, who David knew would surely discover and follow him. And he was right. No sooner had David reached Ramah than Saul did find it out, and sent soldiers to arrest him, but three different bands which he sent, one after another, when they came to the School of Prophets became filled with religious excitement, and neglected their errand. Then Saul himself was frenzied with impatience and started out for Ramah, but before he reached the city, he, too, was overcome by the spirit of religious excitement, and for a day and a night forgot his own errand. So David had time to escape, and went straight back to Saul's court, the place where he had been in such high favour only a short time before. He went to find Jonathan, his friend, who had been eagerly waiting for news of him. The meeting of the youths was a glad one, but there was no time for discussing anything except what David had come to get advice about. At once he asked Jonathan:

"What have I done? What is my sin before your father, that he seeketh my life?"

And Jonathan loved him with a great love and was deeply troubled for his safety, and he answered David:

"God forbid. Thou shalt not die. Behold my father will do nothing either great or small, but he will show it to me, and why should he hide this thing from me? It is not so."

But David knew the truth and he answered:

"Thy father certainly knoweth that I have found favour in thine eyes, and he said 'Let not Jonathan know this lest he be grieved' but truly, as the Lord liveth and as thy soul liveth, there is but a step between me and death."

DAVID THE SHEPHERD BOY

A solemn thing for a young man, so strong, so full of the joy of life, to believe and to say, and as he said it, his voice trembled, and Jonathan's cheeks were white with fear. Only for a moment was Jonathan silent, then looking straight into David's eyes, he said:

"Whatsoever thy soul desireth, I will even do it for thee."

Could there be any better proof of friendship than that?

Then David, who had been thinking what was wisest to do, told Jonathan of the plan which must be carried out in order to find out Saul's intentions with regard to him. There was to be a great festival on the following day, to which Saul had invited David, just as if he and David were on the best of terms, and David told Jonathan that instead of going to the feast, he would hide in a field near by, while Jonathan must go to the feast and see how his absence affected Saul, and also draw him on in every way, to show his feelings for David. Then, as soon as Jonathan had found out his father's feeling towards David, he was to go to the field where David was hiding and shoot three arrows as if shooting at a mark, and send a boy to pick them up. If he should shoot on this side of David's hiding-place, it would mean that David could come out in peace and safety, but if the arrows were shot beyond the place where David was, it would be a sign that he must again flee, for his life would be in danger if he remained.

And so David hid himself in the field and Jonathan went to the feast, as they had planned that he should do, and at first Saul did not notice David's absence, then presently, he asked Jonathan where David was, and Jonathan answered as David had told him to, that David had gone to Bethlehem to attend a family festival there. Then Saul was very angry at both David and Jonathan, and exclaimed:

"Thou hast chosen the son of Jesse to thine own confusion. Surely as long as he liveth, thou shalt not be established in the kingdom. Wherefore, now send for him that he may die."

Although Jonathan was perfectly conscious of his father's bribe of the kingdom should he bring David to be killed, and of the cleverness of Saul's appeal to his desire for power, he had no thought for himself, but only anger that his father could be so hard at heart. But he controlled his temper and merely said:

"Wherefore shall he be slain? What hath he done?"

At this Saul's fury knew no bounds; that he, King of Israel should lose not only his sovereignty, but the loyalty of his own son, because of this lad of Bethlehem, was more than he could bear. With the rage of a frenzied animal, Saul hurled his spear at Jonathan to kill him, but as David had done, Jonathan dodged the deadly weapon, and left the feast, refusing to sit any longer at the table with a father who was so cruel and capricious.

And as soon as possible, Jonathan hastened to David's hiding-place, taking with him his bow and arrows, and a lad to fetch his arrows for him.

And he said to the lad:

"Run, find out the arrows which I shoot!——" and as the lad ran, he shot an arrow beyond him.

And when the lad found the arrow that Jonathan had shot, Jonathan cried after him:

"Is not that the arrow behind thee? Make speed—haste—stay not."

And Jonathan's lad gathered up the arrows and brought them to his master, and he knew nothing about the meaning of that which he had done. Only Jonathan and

DAVID THE SHEPHERD BOY

David knew that, and then because he was eager to be alone with David, Jonathan gave the lad his bow and arrows and bade him take them to the city.

As soon as the lad was out of sight and hearing, David who had heard all that had passed between Jonathan and the boy, came from his hiding-place, and as there was no one to see or hear them, those lads of Israel in that far off land, sat together and talked as lads of to-day might talk, while the sun was sinking low in the west, although by doing so, they took a very great risk should they be found together. But both of them were forgetful of all but the joy of being together. Then with slow step and arm linked in arm, they walked together to the spot where David had been in hiding, and with a quick realisation of the danger ever shadowing David's life, both boys were overcome by the depth of their affection for each other, and by the fear that something was going to part them, and in the custom of the Orient at that time, they clasped hands and made a solemn covenant, or vow, of eternal friendship and mutual help, to extend after the death of either to their descendants.

It was indeed a solemn moment, and the deepest feeling in the boyish hearts was stirred when they made their vow under the wide blue sky, and looked long and sadly into each other's eyes. Then Jonathan said to David:

"Go in peace because we have sworn, both of us, in the name of the Lord, saying, 'The Lord be between me and thee, and between my seed and thy seed for ever;' and then, with a lingering good-bye, Jonathan went back to his home, with a heart aching, not only with loneliness for David, but full of fear of what he would have to suffer and bear in the coming days, and of regret for that weakness of character which he knew his father had allowed to go beyond his own control. And David went to Nob, a city north of Jerusalem, where there was at that time the chief place of worship of the Israelites, and where David naturally turned his steps for instructions and also for food. The story of his flight had not reached the little town among the hills, and he was received with the honour due to the King's son-in-law, although Ahimeleck, the chief priest, was astonished that he came without an armourbearer or a retinue of attendants. Seeing his surprise, David pretended to have come on urgent, secret business for Saul, and begged for food. The priest, believing this, felt that he must treat him with all possible honour, and as there was no other food ready, gave him the bread which was for use on the altar. Meanwhile, David's quick eye had caught a glimpse of a face staring at him through the cracks in the simple forest building. It was Doeg, the Edomite, Saul's savage herdsman, who David felt sure had recognised him. A chill of foreboding crept over David and made him at once demand arms from the peaceful priest. There were none to give except Goliath's sword, which David had taken from the giant when he killed him, and which had been there at Nob, wrapped in a cloth, ever since. With eager joy, David exclaimed:

"There is none like *that,* give it to me!" and seizing the matchless weapon, he fled with it, knowing that Doeg was even then hastening to Saul with news of his whereabouts, and that soon Saul's messengers would be in hot pursuit of him. His next move was a bold one. Leaving Nob, he and his few followers struck across the country in a southwesterly direction, keeping well within the dense forests, until they looked down on the city of Gath. David's condition was desperate now and he resorted to desperate measures. The nearest Philistine city was Gath;

DAVID THE SHEPHERD BOY

the glen where he had killed the giant was close beside him. It was a dangerous thing to trust himself in Gath with Goliath's sword dangling in his belt but David was nothing if not courageous. Danger in some form he must face, the Israelites were behind, the Philistines before him, and he made the plunge and took refuge in Gath. But the move was a fatal one, his identity was at once discovered, to have his life he resorted to the least heroic trick of his whole life. Pretending to be a madman, he raved and stormed and twisted about with horrible contortions, pounded upon the gates of the city, let the spittle run down on his beard, and acted his insane part so perfectly that he completely deceived the King, who laughed at the report that this was David, the Israelite, and ordered him sent from the city, saying that there were enough madmen in it for all practical uses.

David's hasty flight ends this episode and we can fancy his sigh of relief when he had once again escaped so narrowly from danger.

Once more a fugitive, and a real outlaw now, he took refuge in the cave of Adullam, where as soon as it became known that he had taken up an outlaw's life, he was at once joined by a number of men who for some reason were either discontented with their position at court, or fugitives from justice, and had trust in David's ability to achieve victories over enemies and circumstances. Even his own brothers, who had hated and envied him in his earlier days, and his parents, who were now old and feeble, came to join his band of followers, and soon he was the chief of a band numbering about four hundred outlaws, among them some famous warriors who later became noted captains in his army, after he became King of Israel.

Although the wild, free life of the forest was what exactly suited David's own youth and vigour, he felt that his parents were too infirm to bear it, and with characteristic thoughtfulness, he went at once to the King of Moab and begged him to give a home to the old people until he should have a safer place of shelter for them. David's grandmother was Ruth the Moabitess, which according to the rule of Eastern hospitality, entitled all her relations to whatever aid they needed from any of the tribe of Moab, and so the King of Moab cordially assented to David's request, and received Jesse and his wife as inmates of his home.

Among David's first followers were some clever warriors of the tribe of Gad, men fierce in war, and strong and swift of foot. With him also was the prophet Gad himself, and there were even some men from the tribe of Benjamin, the tribe to which King Saul belonged, who joined David's company. It seems to have been a peculiarity of the Benjamites that they could use either hand with equal skill, and those who joined David were armed with bows, and were very valuable allies because they could use both the right hand and the left at once in hurling stones, and shooting arrows, and never miss their aim. At first David feared treachery from these Benjamites, but when he asked them frankly what their intentions were, they said:

"We are thine, David, peace be unto thee and thy helpers, for thy God helpeth thee." Then David received them, and made them captains of his army, and they became enthusiastic admirers of their young leader, as were all David's band.

One incident shows what passionate affection his men felt for him. Saul's army in losing David had lost the one captain who could keep the Philistines in check, and they were over-running the country in numerous bands, having

DAVID THE SHEPHERD BOY

their headquarters in the valley of Rephaim, near Jerusalem. One night, in a moment of fond recollection of a happier past, David cried out in an intense longing for a drink of water from the well near the gate of Bethlehem by which he had often driven his sheep in his younger days. At once, three of his men, without telling him what they were going to do, forced a passage through the Philistine lines and brought him the water for which he longed. Touched by the act, but always modest, David refused to allow men to risk their lives simply for his gratification and poured out the water as a sacrifice to God, according to the religious ceremony of that time, for it was as good as blood, David said, and the three men who brought it to him were afterwards counted among the mightiest of his heroes.

Besides these men, all the others of his little band were devoted to him, seeing his courage and his unconditional dependence on God under all circumstances. The wild, rough life brought out all the manhood there was in his little band of outlaw warriors who were occupied mainly in guerilla warfare with marauding tribes and in eluding the pursuit of Saul, and in this way several years passed, during which time, David's life was full of stirring events, but many a night as he wandered underneath the stars, his thoughts turned in passionate longing to Jonathan, for whom his heart cried out—for Jonathan, whose life was as different from David's, for he had all the comforts of luxurious living, and all the elegance and pomp which were the natural surroundings of a King's son. And yet he was far from happy, for he too longed for David, and he was obliged to spend a large part of his time in watching over his father, whose weakness of character he understood perfectly, and to keep the King from dangerous acts and damaging outbursts of temper, required all of young Jonathan's tact, and most of his time and strength.

Meanwhile, the prophet Gad whose advice was supposed to be divinely inspired, told David that it was no longer safe to remain in the cave of Adullam, so the little band of outlaws left the place where they had been for so long encamped and as outlaws have always done, they took refuge in a forest, somewhere among the hills of Judah.

It was now the end of harvest time in May, and news was brought to David that the town of Keilah was being harassed by plundering bands of Philistines As the town evidently did not belong to Judah at this time, Saul did not move a finger to protect it, although the enemy had shut up the citizens within their own walls and were robbing the loaded threshing floors outside David deliberated long and prayerfully, together with the priest Abiathar, who was one of his followers, deciding whether he might successfully attack the bands who were robbing Keilah. His men were rather fearful of the enterprise, but when Abiathar decided in favour of it, David's band at once marched over the highlands of Judah, and surprised and defeated the Philistines with great loss, and took much booty. David even established himself in the town, but when Saul discovered that fact, he called out all the forces of Israel, and prepared to besiege David, full of fiendish joy that the prey he had so long sought was in his hands at last, for the capture of four hundred men in a fortress however strong, could only be for his large army, a question of time. All this became known to David, who was warned by Abiathar that the inhabitants of Keilah would be compelled for their own safety to give him up to Saul, and his four hundred men only saved themselves by a hasty flight, breaking up into detachments, and fleeing

DAVID THE SHEPHERD BOY

wherever they could go, while David with only a handful of his army, made his way once again into the hospitable wilderness which stretches from the hills of Judah to the shores of the Dead Sea, and there he hid in secret places among the crags and tangled brush, while with fiendish perseverance, Saul sought him every day. But every day God saved him from capture, yet as th days passed he became weary and discouraged in heart. Then in a lonely hour there came a rare joy to David—Jonathan, his friend, stood beside him with outstretched hands and beaming eyes, joy expressed on every line of his sensitive, delicate face.

David has no words ready for such a joyous moment— he is no longer the brave warrior—leader of men. He throws his arms about Jonathan's neck, and tears come,—yes, tears,—and Jonathan too, is unnerved, but there is no time to lose, they may be discovered any moment and that will mean death for at least one of them. Jonathan is the first to speak, clasping David's hand closely.

"Fear not," he says in a clear, calm voice, "the hand of Saul, my father, shall not find thee, and thou shalt be King over Israel, and I shall be next unto thee, and that also my father knoweth."

So spoke Jonathan, and the words came from his heart, for knowing as he did of all the courageous acts of David, and of all the diplomacy he had used to help others as well as himself, Jonathan's heart told him that his friend was truly worthy to be King of Israel rather than he, the rightful heir to the throne, and with deepest love and admiration in his eyes and voice, and at peril of his life, should he be found with David, he told David this, and David's eyes shone with joy and pride in his friend's appreciation, and his hand-clasp grew firmer, and there was deep, intense silence while the two friends thought of past and future, and looked into each other's eyes as comrades look who trust and understand.

Then, Jonathan renewed his covenant of friendship for David, and of loyalty to his descendants for ever, and David began to give his answering promise, but he could not finish the words because of a great sob which burst from him. And Jonathan could say no words of comfort, for his soul was full of misery too, because he must so soon part from David. Then David who was quick to see and feel Jonathan's pain, turned away, and hastily, with a mighty effort controlled his misery, that his friend might not see sorrow on his face, and with one last look Jonathan turned and silently went from the forest, out into the larger world and back into the less free life that was his at the Court of his father. Back to his own duty which he never shirked, went Jonathan, and to David remained only the fulfilling of that renewed covenant of comradeship. And fulfil it he did.

In the following months Saul still sought daily to kill him, but daily failed to do so, and instead David had an opportunity to capture and kill Saul, when he came upon him by night sleeping, with his spear stuck in the ground at his head, and surrounded by Abner and his people who were sleeping too. Think what a temptation that was for David to resist! But even though it would have freed his life of a dangerous enemy and raised him to the throne, David would not yield to it, for he said:

"Who can stretch forth his hand against the Lord's anointed and be guiltless? The Lord shall smite him, or his day will come to die, or he will descend into the battle and perish, but God forbid that I should stretch my hand against him."

DAVID THE SHEPHERD BOY

And never did he raise his hand against Saul, though still Saul pursued him with relentless hatred, but still David escaped from his hand, and he and his band of followers became daily more famous for their deeds of valour, and for the brave warfare they waged against their enemies.

War again broke out between the Israelites and the Philistines. David and his men who were not now with either army, but who had just captured the Amalekites and taken from them large booty, were rejoicing over this victory, when joy was turned to sorrow. News was brought to David that both Saul and Jonathan had fallen in battle against the Philistines at Gilboa.

Jonathan gone from him! Jonathan, his friend, gone beyond his sight for ever! David refused to believe this until he who brought the sad tidings had again and again given proof of its truth. Then David gave way to his grief, and he and all his men who sorrowed with him, wept and mourned and fasted until evening, for Saul, the king, and for Jonathan, his son, and David mourned as one who cannot be comforted.

Although David had known only too well the truth about Saul's great weakness, and had feared him as his most dangerous enemy, still to him was Saul always the King of Israel, mighty in strength of character, and in all the pomp and power of a nation's ruler; still the king of a shepherd boy's dreams and also he was the father of Jonathan, and because of David's childhood's ideal of Saul, the king, and because of his great grief for Jonathan his friend, David, who was now the King of Israel, expressed his true feelings in this wonderful poem in memory of Saul, and of Jonathan his friend:

TEN BOYS FROM HISTORY

The beauty of Israel is slain upon thy high places
How are the mighty fallen!
Tell it not in Gath
Publish it not in the streets of Askelon,
Lest the daughters of the Philistines rejoice
Lest the daughters of the uncircumcised triumph,
Ye mountains of Gelboa, let there be no dew,
Neither let there be rain upon you!
For there the shield of the mighty was vilely cast away,
The shield of Saul, the anointed of the Lord.
From the blood of the slain,
From the fat of the mighty,
The bow of Jonathan turned not back
And the sword of Saul returned not empty,
Jonathan and Saul
Were lovely and pleasant in their lives
And in their deaths they were not divided;
They were swifter than eagles,
They were stronger than lions,
Ye daughters of Israel, weep over Saul,
Who clothed you in scarlet, with other delights,
Who put on ornaments of gold on your apparel,
How are the mighty fallen in the midst of the battle!
O Jonathan, thou wast slain
I am distressed for thee, my brother Jonathan!
Very pleasant hast thou been unto me,
Thy love to me was wonderful,
Passing the love of women,
How are the mighty fallen,
And the weapons of war perished!

LOUIS SEVENTEENTH:
The Boy King Who Never Reigned

LOUIS SEVENTEENTH:
The Boy King Who Never Reigned

IT was the early morning of a bright June day, and the famous gardens surrounding the palace at Versailles were gay with bloom and heavy with scents as rare as was the morning. King Louis Sixteenth of France looked from a window out over the terraces in their vari-coloured beauty, and saw among the blossoms, a little figure busy with spade and rake, and although the King's heart was heavy with sorrow because of the death of his elder son, the Dauphin, as the eldest son of the King of France, and heir to the throne, was always called, yet he was filled too with pride as he looked out at the little Louis Charles, to whom only three short hours before had descended the titles and honours which had belonged to his brother.

The King's long and earnest glance at the little Dauphin attracted the child's attention, and dropping his tools, he waved frantically towards the window, crying out:

"Papa, see the beautiful flowers. I am pleased with myself. I shall deserve mamma's first kiss to-day. I shall have a bouquet for her dressing-table. May I come and show it to you?"

The king bowed his head in answer and smiled a sad smile as he turned to the queen, Marie Antoinette, who even then stood beside him, weeping bitterly for the other son who had gone from her for ever.

So absorbed was King Louis in his attempt to comfort her, that he forgot the new little Dauphin, until the door opened softly, and he saw the small figure standing just inside the door, holding tightly in his hand a bouquet of violets and roses. Charming in his childish grace and beauty was little Louis as he stood there, watching his father and then his mother, with grave concern at their evident sadness, and quickly he held up his flowers to his mother and said with sweet grace:

"Mamma, I have picked you some flowers from my garden."

Still Marie Antoinette could not speak, but the king caught the child up in his arms, saying:

"Marie, he too is our son. He is the Dauphin of France."

Slowly Marie Antoinette turned, clasped his bright, lovely face in her two hands, and stooping, kissed him tenderly on his forehead.

"I had forgotten," she said. "God bless and protect you, Dauphin of France. I only pray that the storm clouds which now darken our sky may be long past, when you ascend the throne of your fathers!"

Little Louis' forehead was wrinkled with perplexity.

"But, mamma," he asked timidly—"why is it you all call me Dauphin to-day, when I am just your little Louis, who is called the Duke of Normandy?"

"My son," said the King, solemnly, "each day differs from the last, and this new day has brought you a new name and a new position. Your poor dear brother has left us for ever. He has gone to God, and you are now in his place, the Dauphin of France."

"And is that why mamma is crying, and will Louis never come back?"

LOUIS THE DAUPHIN

"No, dear, he will never come back, and so your mamma is grieving."

Quickly little Louis' arms went around her neck.

"Oh," he cried, "poor, dear mamma! I don't see how anyone can leave you, and not come back? *I* will never leave you, never, never!"

"God grant it!" sighed the queen, pressing him tenderly to her. "May He grant it—oh, my precious child!" and then with his face close to hers, and a little hand held tight in the big one of his father, whose arm was around them both, Louis continued:

"If it is mine now, please tell me what it means—that name, the Dauphin."

The king answered:

"My son, this is what it means. You are now the eldest son of the King of France, and some day you will be the king, and to you belong now the titles and honours that were your brother's. Do you understand?"

Instead of showing appreciation, Louis' blue eyes looked entreatingly at the Queen, and his lips quivered.

"Mamma," he whispered, "I like being Duke of Normandy best. Will you love me any better if I am called the Dauphin?"

"No, dear child," answered the Queen tenderly, "I shall not love you better, but you are no longer the Duke of Normandy. You are the Dauphin now, the future King of France!" A sob choked the words as Marie Antoinette turned hastily away to hide her grief, and in doing so, she put her foot on the flowers which little Louis had brought her. His face clouded as he saw this, then with a bright smile he looked into the Queen's face, saying quickly:

"Mamma, I wish you always walked on flowers I picked for you."

Without a word Marie Antoinette turned, and clasping him in her arms, was comforted. Then, reminded of state duties to be done, she was about to release him when he whispered:

"Did my poor dear brother only leave me his title? Oh, mamma, I do not want it. But there is something of his that I *do* want to have very, very much now that I am the Dauphin."

The King looked bewildered, but the Queen smiled through her tears.

"I think I can guess what it is," she said, "see if I can, little Louis," and putting him down, she softly left the room, and when she came back there ran and frisked about her, jumping for joy of comradeship, a tiny black dog who rushed up to Louis, and jumped on him over and over again, and the child clasped it in his arms, while the dog put its paws on Louis' shoulders and licked his rosy cheeks with frantic affection.

"Now, my Louis," asked the Queen, "did I guess right? Wasn't that what you wanted so much?"

"Oh, yes it was! It was!" exclaimed the boy, his eyes shining with joy. "Is he really mine now? Does he belong to my inheritance?"

The Queen could not answer, but the King spoke sadly.

"Yes, my son, he belongs to your inheritance."

The Dauphin shouted with joy.

"He is mine! He is mine!" and as he held the little dog close to him, the picture was a pretty one, the boy with his round rosy face, dimpled chin and deep blue eyes shaded by long, dark lashes, with his high forehead, and heavy golden hair, all the delicacy of his colouring and features thrown into relief by the dark blue velvet of his suit, all the charm of his expressive face shone in his joy over the new treasure which he was clasping tight. What

LOUIS THE DAUPHIN

to the little Dauphin was the silver star embroidered on his left shoulder, which showed his princely rank and removed him from the rank and file of other boys? What was a crown, a title—even the throne itself? They were less than nothing to him in comparison with the little dog nestling in his arms and licking his face, and while the King and Queen watched the pretty picture they sighed for the simple joys of childhood, and Marie Antoinette, looking into her husband's face murmured:

"God keep him in His care!"

Although the little Louis' new title was of such small value to him, yet the possession of it changed the whole of his life, and as soon as he became the Dauphin, his education and training were of the gravest importance, for he would some day rule in his father's place.

Accordingly, every possible advantage that could be given him was secured, and while his father saw to it that he should have enough out-of-door exercise to keep him sturdy and strong, his mother superintended his lessons, as well as those of his sister, Thérèse. Although Marie Antoinette was young and pleasure-loving and was often called frivolous because of the spontaneous gaiety into which her nature often led her, yet she was a devoted mother, and every morning at ten o'clock, Thérèse, the Dauphin, and their teachers went to the queen's rooms, and there learned and recited lessons.

The little Dauphin was a brilliant scholar and said such bright things that all the courtiers took great pleasure in asking him questions, that they might hear his answers. One day while saying his lessons, he began to hiss loudly, for which his mother reproved him.

"I was only hissing at myself," he said, "because I just said my lesson so badly."

On the evening before the queen's birthday the king

told the Dauphin that he would buy him a handsome bouquet to give his mother for a birthday present, but that he wanted him to write a letter of congratulation to go with it. To his surprise the Dauphin did not show as much pleasure as he expected at this, and finally on questioning him he discovered the truth.

"I have got a beautiful everlasting in my garden," Louis said, "I want to give it to her, please, papa, it will be my bouquet and my letter all together, for when I give it to mamma I shall say, 'I hope mamma, that you will be like this flower.'"

The idea was so pretty and the boy so eager, that he had his way, and King Louis' pride in this clever child was great.

He was no prig, no saintly child, this little King Louis Seventeenth to be, he was just a sensitive, affectionate boy, whose winning manner and charm of person attracted all to him, and made him an especial pet of the older people from whose conversation he gathered much information which they never thought he understood.

One day when playing in the garden, full of excited vigour, he was just going to rush through a hedge of roses, when an attendant stopped him and warned him, saying:

"Monseigneur, one of those thorns might blind you or tear your face."

But the Dauphin persisted, and when halfway through the hedge, called back:

"Thorny paths lead to glory"—a phrase so ominous of the poor little Dauphin's future that it has ever been remembered as one of the most remarkable of his sayings.

For some time, the Dauphin who was quick to respond to joy or sadness in those around him noticed many signs of distress, not only in the faces of his father and mother, but

LOUIS THE DAUPHIN

in those of others whom he saw daily, and many an hour when no one knew it, his childish mind spent in wondering about the situation, trying to understand the heated words he heard, the tears he saw, and sometimes he would creep up to Marie Antoinette and pat her smooth cheek reassuringly, and kiss her lovingly, and though this comforted, it added to the pain of the Queen, who feared for the happiness of the future King of France.

The Reign of Terror was at hand. The Revolutionists, fierce and strong in their murderous frenzy had risen, risen to kill monarchs and monarchy. Louis Sixteenth was on the throne—therefore Louis Sixteenth must go; Marie Antoinette was his wife; she had danced, and spent money like water while they, the people had needed bread, so they said—and Marie Antoinette must go. Little Louis was heir to the throne—that throne whose power must be overthrown, and so Louis the Dauphin must go.

The rulers of France had for generations proved so false to their trust and to their kingly responsibility that the love of the people had at last been changed into hate. Louis Fourteenth and Louis Fifteenth had sinned so deeply against those whom their oath of office bound them to protect, that now at last there was no feeling but revenge and hatred in the hearts of the subjects of the King of France, and on the heads of the reigning sovereigns, Louis Sixteenth and Marie Antoinette fell the horrors of the Reign of Terror, which was now reaching a point where only torture and bloodshed could appease the fiends who were rapidly becoming all-powerul. It was claimed that the taxes collected from the people for the expenses of war and government were being misused for the extravagances and frivolities of the royal family. It was even claimed that the people were starving for bread while the King and

Queen were living in luxury, and this because the fiends of the revolution had caused all bake-shops to stop baking bread, so that the cry of starvation might be raised among the people, who could then be incited to storm the palace and demand bread of the royal family.

The very scum of civilisation, the dregs of the population of France, were roused in fierce and unjust revolt against the royal family; yes, in revolt and in power, and on a day of early October, 1789, a howling mob of frenzied men, women and children swept up the peaceful avenues of Versailles, shrieking their fiendish cries for vengeance on the royal family, and then they invaded and took possession of the royal apartments. Aghast at the outrages committed in the name of the French people, the King and Queen tried in every way to restore the mob to peace, but in vain. The leaders of the rebellion demanded the immediate appearance in Paris, which was the seat of the revolution, of King Louis and his family, where they could be closely watched by their enemies, describing in alarming terms, the danger to his majesty if he did not comply with the request. Accordingly, after hours of indescribable horrors and humiliation and anguish, the king was obliged to give his consent to the plan, and the royal family made ready for their departure from Versailles. During their seven hours' journey to Paris, they were followed by a rabble of such human fiends as had invaded the palace at Versailles, and although throughout the whole terrible trip, Marie Antoinette and the King bore themselves with sad and dignified composure, yet the strain on them both was almost too great to be borne. Through all the agony and excitement, the Dauphin frightened though he was, seeing his mother's tears, tried to smile courageously into her face, and to keep back words of com-

LOUIS THE DAUPHIN

plaint, and the sight of his courage almost broke his mother's heart. What would this all mean to him, the future king of France? Alas, poor little Dauphin!

At last they reached the Tuileries, the royal palace in Paris, where no French King had lived since Louis Fifteenth was a young man. There had been no preparations made for the coming of the royal family. The palace, so long uninhabited was in a state of dilapidation, and there were no comforts in it, and very few necessities. But the travellers were too much exhausted to heed anything but that they had reached a temporary shelter and were relieved that death, which the day before had seemed so imminent, had been, for the present, put aside.

Exhausted to the breaking point, Marie Antoinette slept soundly that night, and on the next morning as she sipped her chocolate in a room which had been hastily transformed into a sitting-room for her, she was thinking sadly of life and its changes when the door opened and the Dauphin ran in and flung himself into her arms.

"Oh, mamma," he cried, " please let us go back to our beautiful palace at home. This big house frightens me with its shadows. Why have we come here, mamma, when we have such a lovely palace and garden of our own?"

The queen sighed.

" My son," she said, " this palace belongs to us too, as well as Versailles, and it is considered a beautiful palace. It is where the great Louis Fourteenth lived, you know."

"Well, I don't like it at all and I wish we could go away," whispered the Dauphin, casting a homesick look around the great bare room, furnished so meagrely with faded furniture.

" I wish so too." The queen scarcely breathed the

words, but the sensitive child's ears caught them, and he answered eagerly.

"Then why do we have to stay? I thought a queen could always do what she wanted to do."

In answer the poor, sore-hearted queen burst into tears, whereupon the Dauphin's tutor tried to take the child from her, saying severely:

"My prince, you see you trouble the queen, and her majesty sorely needs a rest. Come with me for a walk."

But Marie Antoinette shook her head and clung to the child whose hand was now gently stroking her cheek, and whose tears were mingled with her own.

Then from the street came the dreaded sound of loud shouts and cries and threats, and the Dauphin clung more tightly to his mother, both shivering with dread but both brave.

"Mamma," asked the Dauphin, "is to-day going to be just like yesterday?"

His question was answered by the king himself, who entered the room just then and flung himself into a chair, telling the queen that those who had aided the mob in their violent acts were about to be brought to trial for them, and he added his request that the queen should receive the committee who had come to judge the people for their violence.

In stately dignity, Marie Antoinette then left the room to receive other subjects, who still considered her the queen of France, and after her going, King Louis and his little son were left alone.

The king, exhausted in body and mind, closed his eyes and lay back in his chair, ready to sink into a light doze, when he was roused by a gentle touch on his arm.

Beside him stood the Dauphin, his great blue eyes full

of grave thoughtfulness. When he saw the King's eyes open, he spoke.

"Papa," he said, hesitatingly, "I should like to ask you something—something really serious!"

"Something really serious!" replied the King, smiling in spite of himself. "Well, what is it? Let me hear."

"Papa," answered the Dauphin, with an air of one who has thought deeply on a subject. "My governess has always told me I must love the people of France and treat them kindly, because they love you and mama so much. But if they do, papa, then why do the people act so badly to you? And oh, papa, I have been told that your people owe you obedience and respect, but they were not obedient nor respectful yesterday and they said dreadful things I never heard before. What does it mean, papa?"

The king drew the child on to his knee and put an arm around the grave little questioner, telling him that he would explain it to him, but that he would have to listen carefully if he wished to understand such grave matters.

"Oh, I will, I will," answered the Dauphin eagerly. "I know that I am one of your subjects, and that as your son and a subject too, I must give a good example to the French people of loving and obeying the king. But it seems that my example has not done any good at all yet. How does that happen, papa?"

In answer, the King told him that wicked men had said to the people that he did not love them, that they had listened and believed this, that France had had great wars, and wars cost a great deal. And so, because he was the King, he had asked money of his subjects, just as had always been done by other Kings.

"Oh, but papa," cried the Dauphin, "why did you do that? Why did you not take my purse and pay out of that?

You know that I receive every day my purse filled with bright new francs and I could have helped you easily. And, oh papa, do your people have more money than you have yourself?"

King Louis answered that a king receives all his money from the people, but gives it all back to them again, that he governs those people, and they owe him respect and obedience and have to pay taxes to him, and so if he needs money he raises it by laying extra taxes upon them. Then he asked, "do you understand that, little Louis?"

"Oh, yes, indeed!" The Dauphin was breathless with interest now. "I have been told about that, but I don't like it. It seems to me that if a man is the king, he ought to have all the money and give it to the people when they need it. They ought to ask him for it, not he ask them."

To this the king agreed, but added with a sigh, that kings had so misused their power and authority that the people no longer trusted them, and that now a king could not pay out money unless the people knew what it was to be used for, and were willing.

"Have you used people's money, papa, without asking their leave?" cried Louis eagerly. "Was that why they came to Versailles yesterday and were so wicked to us? For those bad men and women were the people, weren't they?"

King Louis shook his head. "No, my son," he said. "The people can not come to me in such great masses. They have to send representatives. Those representatives I called to me at Versailles and asked of them money for the outlays I had to make, but they asked things in return, of me which I could not grant, either for my own sake or for yours, my son, who are some day to be my successor. Then the people were led to believe that I did not love them, but I am determined to show them that I do love them and am ready to share everything with them. That is why we have left lovely Versailles and come to live here, where we have to do without so much that we enjoy. And we must try to be contented here and share all the disagreeable things that the people have to bear, which is what a true King should do."

The Dauphin had sat like an old man, listening, and now as his father stopped speaking, the boy laid a hand on his breast, saying solemnly:

"Papa, I have understood everything, and I am very much ashamed that I complained at all. And I promise you I will take pains to give everybody a good example. I will be happy and contented here."

And the Dauphin kept his word; he took pains to be contented, and never said another word about Versailles, but tried to get all the pleasure he could from the dreary old palace and its garden, so different from that at Versailles, where the Dauphin had so much ground in which to work. Here in the garden, there was only one small corner set aside for the use of the royal family. This was surrounded by iron palings, through which faces full of hate and malice would often peer at the little Dauphin while he was busy gardening. One day he heard such words and saw such threatening faces that he shrank back and ran to his mother, who comforted him as best she could and said that he must be brave and strong, or she would cry too, and that she must not do this because it was exactly what the men who were trying to hurt their feelings, wanted to see her do.

The boy's eyes flashed.

"I will never complain again," he cried, "and they shall never again have the pleasure of seeing you or me cry if I can help it. But, mamma, tell me—are there no good men in the world?"

"Yes, Louis," answered the queen. "You must believe that all men are good and treat them courteously, until you have proved the contrary. If they refuse your friendly kindness, it will not be your fault, and you will have done what is right, no matter what others do."

A shadow passed over the child's lovely face.

"But, mamma," he said, "all men are not good. The men who abused and cursed us so were not good, and I could never be friendly to them, never!"

"We will hope that we shall never see them again," said the queen, "and I wish you to be so kind and polite to everyone who comes here, that all men may admire and respect their future king, even though he is still a child."

"I will be," cried the boy with spirit, "so that you may be satisfied with me, mamma. Just for that I will be so!"

As Marie Antoinette was kissing the pretty boy who was her comforter, the mayor of Paris and General Lafayette were announced, and the Dauphin whispered to his mother:

"That general was at Versailles with the bad men. I can *never* be kind to him."

"Hush," whispered the Queen—"For God's sake, do not let anybody hear that. No—no—he does not belong to our enemies. He wishes us well. Treat him kindly, my child."

And then Marie Antoinette took her son by the hand, and together they met their distinguished guests, who had come with the unwelcome news that, according to the old custom of the days of Henry the Fourth, the people wished to have free access to the gardens of the Tuileries, which freedom had been denied them since the coming of King Louis and his family.

LOUIS THE DAUPHIN

The queen was bitterly opposed to this, for it meant that, for her own comfort and protection, she must only walk in the garden at certain times and under escort, and she was speaking with proud and angry fearlessness to the general about the matter, when the Dauphin left her side and running forward, extended his hand to Lafayette, crying:

"General, I should like to salute you. Mamma told me I must be polite and kind to all who are good to us, and she said that you wish us well. Let me, therefore, greet you kindly, and give you my hand."

As he spoke, he raised his blue eyes and looked smilingly and trustingly into those of the general and then at his mother; and his hearer, whose heart had just kindled with anger against Marie Antoinette and her rebellious words, felt anger melt into admiration, together with reverence and astonishment at the words of the manly little Dauphin. Bending his knee, in stately grace, he pressed the Dauphin's small hand to his lips and said gravely as to a comrade:

"My prince, you have spoken as with the tongue of an angel, and I swear to you and to your royal mother that I will never forget this moment. The kiss I have impressed upon the hand of my future king is at once the seal of a solemn vow and the oath of unchangeable fidelity and devotion to my king and the royal family. Dauphin of France, you have to-day gained a soldier for your throne who is prepared to shed his last drop of blood for you and your house, and on whose loyalty you may always count."

General Lafayette had tears in his eyes, and his noble face glowed with emotion, while the child before him looked at him with wistful eyes and a happy smile. Close by stood Marie Antoinette, her air of proud defiance turned to one of gentle sweetness. She knew what that moment meant in the history of France, and her heart thrilled with pride in her little son, the Dauphin. Stooping, she kissed his golden hair, and then, without an attempt to conceal the emotion, she finished her conversation with the general and mayor, and then, making her adieus to them beckoned to the Dauphin to go with her from the pavilion in which the interview had taken place, and to return to the palace.

Instead of walking beside her, the Dauphin paused and asked:

"Mamma, please let me walk alone. I want the people to see I am not afraid, as they may think if I let you lead me. I want to be like the Chevalier Bayard, that the Abbé talked to me about the other day. I want to be *sans peur et sans reproche*—like Bayard."

The queen smiled through tears.

"Very well, my chevalier," she said. "You shall walk alone."

"And before you, please. The knights always walk in advance of the ladies, to protect them from danger. I am your knight, mamma, and I want to be, as long as I live." And he added with a pretty, playful bow, "Will you allow it, my royal lady?"

"I allow it! So go in front, chevalier, little Louis. We will take the same way we came."

The Dauphin sprang along the path for quite a distance, when he stopped suddenly and turned round to the queen, who with her two footmen was walking quietly behind him.

"Well, Chevalier Bayard, what are you stopping for?" asked the queen with a smile.

LOUIS THE DAUPHIN

"I am waiting for you," he said gravely, "because this is where my knightly service commences, for it is here that danger begins."

"It is true," said the Queen, and even as she spoke, there came to her ears a sound of shouting as loud as the booming of cannon. "Oh, my child," cried Marie Antoinette, "the sound is like the thundering of a storm at sea! But such storms lie in God's hand and He protects those who trust Him. Think of that, little Louis, and do not be afraid!"

"Oh, I am not afraid!" cried Louis, running happily on. And yet, outside the fence behind which they were walking, was a dense mass of angry people muttering curses on the queen and the Dauphin.

All at once, the mother's heart almost stopped beating from fright and horror. A man had extended his bare, powerful arm through the paling of the fence, to bar the Dauphin's way when he should try to pass it.

The boy saw the arm, hesitated a little, then went bravely forward. The queen hurried that she might be near him when he reached the danger point. On walked the Dauphin in proud courage. On hurried the queen and as she reached him, she cried:

"Come here, my son. Give me your hand."

But instead of responding to her cry, the little prince sprang forward and stood directly in front of the outstretched arm, and reaching out his small white hand, laid it on the brown clenched fist that had been ready to clutch him as in a vise, while a chorus of cheers at his courage went up from outside the wall.

"Good-day, sir," he said in a loud voice, "Good-day!" As he spoke he took hold of the great rough hand and shook it.

Little fool," roared the man, "what do you mean, and how dare you lay your puny paw in the claws of a lion?"

The Dauphin smiled. "Sir, I thought you were stretching out your hand to reach me with it, and so I give you mine and say good-day, sir!"

"And if I wanted, I could crush your fingers with my fist," cried the man, still holding the little hand firmly.

But from a hundred throats outside the fence came the cry "You shall not do it, Simon. You shall not hurt the boy!"

"Who can hinder me if I choose to do it?" asked the cobbler, whose name was Simon, with a coarse laugh. "See, I hold the hand of the future King of France, and I can break it if I choose, and make it so it can never lift the sceptre of France. The little monkey thought he would take hold of my hand and make me draw it back, but now my hand has got hold of his, and holds it fast. And mark this, boy, the time is past when kings seized us and trod us down, now we seize them, and do not let them go unless we will."

"But, Mr. Simon," said Louis, "you see very plainly that I do not want to do any harm, and I know you do not want to do me any harm, and I ask you to be so good as to take away your arm, that my mamma can go on with her walk."

"But suppose I do not do as you want me to?" asked the man defiantly. "I suppose then your mamma would dictate to me, and perhaps call some soldiers and order them to shoot the dreadful people?"

"You know, Master Simon, that I give no such commands and never gave such," said the queen quickly. "The king and I love our people and never would give our soldiers orders to fire on them, and now, sir—the Queen of France and her son will no longer be detained!" With a

LOUIS THE DAUPHIN

quick movement she struck back the arm of the cobbler, Simon, snatched the Dauphin away like lightning and passed by before Simon had time to put his arm back.

The crowd watching were filled with enthusiasm by the courage of the queen. They applauded, laughed and shouted, while the cries, "Long live the Queen! Long live the Dauphin!" passed like wildfire among the throng behind the fence, and although in the eyes of Simon whose evil design had been frustrated by a little child, there still shone hatred, Marie Antoinette, who was now hand in hand with the Dauphin, reached in safety the little garden reserved for the use of the royal family. Once within its iron gate, decorated with the arms of the kings of France, she felt as if all power had gone from her, and she could no longer hide her fear and grief, but, no, she must be cheerful for her son's sake, and her servants must not see her brow clouded, and so, with head erect and flashing eyes, she walked on.

"Mamma," cried the Dauphin, interrupting her thoughts. "There comes the king, my father. He will be glad to hear I was so courageous."

The queen quickly stooped and kissed him. "Yes, truly my little Bayard," she said, "you have done honour to your great example and been really a little chevalier *sans peur et sans reproche,* but remember, Louis, true bravery does not glory in its great deeds and does not wish others to admire them, but keeps silent and leaves others to talk of them!"

"Yes, and I will be silent too," cried Louis, with sparkling eyes. "You will see that I can be silent too," and child though he was, he showed from that moment a quick understanding and appreciation of the humility necessary to real greatness.

TEN BOYS FROM HISTORY

That winter in the Tuileries was a dismal one indeed, for the royal family had none of the gaiety and freedom which had been part of the happy life at Versailles, and even when the King wished to go to his summer palace at St. Cloud for rest and change, this was not allowed. At last, weary of the insults and restraints heaped upon them, the royal family attempted to escape secretly from Paris, but the plot was discovered, their carriages stopped, and they were escorted back to the Tuileries by a shouting shrieking mob of men and women who were fiendishly glad of their capture. After that the King and Queen and the Dauphin were always treated as prisoners in their own palace, with guards set over them to watch their every movement, and the poor little Dauphin could not go out nor play freely and happily as could the poorest peasant child in France. After some months had passed, however, the fury of the people grew somewhat less, and they were allowed to close the doors of their rooms when they wished, and to walk out in the gardens once more. It even seemed for some time as if what King Louis had done to win back the trust of his people had been successful, and that the throne of France might regain its dignity and power before that time when Louis the Dauphin, should come into his inheritance.

He, meanwhile, was filling this period of calm with such affairs as interested and amused him, and his greatest joy was that he was again allowed to work in his garden. Although it was so small in comparison to that at Versailles, it was yet a bit of paradise to him, and as soon as his study hours were over, he always hurried out to dig his ground, and water and pick his blossoms, and it was the great delight of those subjects who loved the manly little fellow, to stand outside the fence and watch him as he worked. The Dauphin was generally accompanied, when

LOUIS THE DAUPHIN

he went outside the palace, by several soldiers from the detachment of the National Guard, who were on duty at the Tuileries, and the boy himself, who was now having military drills, generally wore the uniform of the National Guard, and so charming and so manly was this little National Guardsman of six years, that he became the idol of Paris. Fans and lockets were decorated with his picture, which society women wore, and everywhere the beauty and wit of the little fellow were talked of.

The boys of Paris shared the enthusiasm of their elders, and formed themselves into a regiment, which was called the Regiment of the Dauphin, which, with the king's permission, marched to the Tuileries to parade before the Dauphin. As usual, he was found in his garden, and was anxious to show his treasures to them even before he answered their request that he become Colonel of their regiment. When he accepted the honour urged upon him, one of the officers said:

"But that will mean giving up gathering flowers for your mamma."

"Oh, no," said the Dauphin, quickly, "that will not prevent me from taking care of my flowers. Many of these gentlemen tell me that they, too, have little gardens, and if they love the queen as much as their colonel loves her, mamma will have whole regiments of bouquets every day."

A cheer showed the boys' appreciation of their little colonel's sentiment, and the regiment of the Dauphin became one of the most poular organisations in Paris. Their uniform was a miniature copy of the French guards, with their three-cornered hats and white jackets, and whenever they marched through the Place de la Carousel, the people crowded to see the army of sturdy boys with their handsome little colonel.

TEN BOYS FROM HISTORY

So great was the boys' love for the Dauphin that the officers of the regiment came to the palace one day to make him a present, in the name of the whole regiment, and they were enthusiastically received by their colonel.

"Welcome, my comrades," he cried. "My mamma tells me you have brought me a present. But it gives me such pleasure to see you that nothing more is needed."

"But Colonel, you will not refuse our gift?" said a little officer named Palloy, and he added proudly:

"We bring you a set of dominoes made entirely out of the ruins of the Bastile"*

Taking the wrapper from the white marble box, bound with gold, he gave it to the Dauphin, at the same time reciting the following lines:

"Those glowing walls that once woke our fear
Are changed into the toy we offer here
And when with joyful face the gift you view
Think what the people's love can do."

Joyfully the Dauphin received the beautiful present and listened eagerly to the explanation of how to play the new game. On the back of each domino, in the black marble, was a gold letter, and when the whole set of dominoes was arranged in regular order, they formed this sentence, Vive le Roi, Vive la Reine, et Vive le Dauphin (Long live the King, the Queen and the Dauphin). The marble of the box was taken from the altar-slab in the chapel of the Bastile, and in the middle, in gold relief, was a picture of King Louis.

*The Bastile was the national prison, which had been entirely destroyed by the Revolutionists.

LOUIS THE DAUPHIN

"That is my papa!" cried Louis joyfully, when he saw it.

"Yes," said Palloy. "Every one of us bears him in his heart. And like the King, you will live for the happiness of all, and like him, you will be the idol of France. We who shall one day be French soldiers and citizens, bring to you, who will then be our commander-in-chief and king, our homage as the future supporters of the throne which is destined for you and which the wisdom of your father has placed under the unshakable power of law. The gift which we offer you is small, but each one of us adds his heart to it."

"And I give you all of my heart in return for it," cried the Dauphin, joyfully, " and I shall take great pains to do my lessons well so I may be allowed to amuse myself playing dominoes."

The delight of the Dauphin was so evident that his comrades who had brought him the present felt a keener affection even than before for their little Colonel, and the Queen who had been present during the whole scene spoke in friendly words of thanks to the boys, who then withdrew, escorted by the king and the Dauphin, who had no knowledge, child of destiny that he was, of the omen contained in that present. But Marie Antoinette knew only too well, and her heart was heavy when she saw the present made from the stones of the Bastile. But of this she gave no sign. and from that day attempted more than ever to endear herself and her son to the people who had so little trust in her. One day when a crowd of fiendish women behind the fence called out cruel things about the Queen, the Dauphin could be no longer silent.

"You lie, oh, you lie!" he cried angrily. "My mamma is *not* a wicked woman, and she does not hate the people. She is good. She is so good that—that——" tears choked him, and ashamed to show such signs of weakness, he dashed out of the garden into the palace, but as he reached the queen's apartments he choked back the tears, saying, " I will not cry any more, for that will only trouble mamma and I can see she has trouble enough without that. I will laugh and sing and jump about, and then she may smile a little instead of crying, as I often find her doing."

His tutor, the Abbé Davout, heartily approved of this, and the Dauphin sprang into his mother's presence with a merry smile which gladdened the queen's heart and made her forget her sorrows for awhile. This pleased the Dauphin greatly, and he re-doubled his efforts to be merry, making the little dog stand on its hind legs, while Louis put on its black head a paper cap which he had made, painted with red stripes, like those worn by the Jacobins or Revolutionists and cried:

"Monsieur Jacobi, behave respectfully. Make your salutations to her majesty, the Queen!"

He was rewarded by a hug and a kiss from the Queen and then ran off with the dog barking at his heels.

Little Louis was, as we have seen, an eager and brilliant scholar and one day he begged the Abbé to give him lessons in grammar which he had begun to learn some time before.

"Gladly," answered the Abbé, "your last lesson, if I remember rightly, was upon the three degrees of comparison—the positive, the comparative and the superlative. But you must have forgotten all that."

"You are mistaken," answered the Dauphin, "and I will prove it to you. Listen:—the positive is when I say, 'my Abbé is a kind Abbé'; the comparative is when I say 'my Abbé is kinder than another Abbé,' and the superla-

LOUIS THE DAUPHIN

tive," he continued, looking at the Queen who was listening —" is when I say, 'mamma is the kindest and most amiable of all mammas!'"

The retort was so clever, the manner of saying it so charming, that the Abbé and Marie Antoinette exchanged glances of amusemen and pride, but the little prince was unconscious of having said or done anything unusual.

Besides grammar, Louis studied Italian, which he could speak and read fluently; he also studied Latin, and some of the sentences he translated have been preserved, such as "True friends are useful to princes." "I know a prince who easily flies into a passion." "Flatterers are very dangerous to princes." From these sentences it is evident that the Abbé was trying to teach his clever little scholar more than one thing at a time. Louis was also taught arithmetic, geometry and geography, this last by means of a huge hollow globe lit by a lantern, which had been invented for the special use of the Dauphin, by a celebrated professor in the University of Paris. Louis also was trained in all sorts of athletic sports and when he was seven years old was sturdy of body and far more mature of mind than many older boys. At seven, according to the court custom of France, he was obliged to be given into the care of a governor. The people wished to choose this governor and named several candidates who were utterly unworthy of the position, but they were obliged to set aside their wishes and accept a man named by the king, who also himself continued to superintend his son's education.

At this time the clouds of political disaster were again hanging over the palace, and even the Dauphin could see and feel the uneasiness that surrounded him.

On June 20, 1792, King Louis refused to sign two decrees which the people wished him to sign, and with his refusal the storm of riot and revolution burst forth again. An immense mob of shrieking, howling people stormed the Tuileries, where no measures had been taken in defence, and the king gave orders that the doors of the palace be flung open and the people be allowed to pass in unhindered. In a few minutes every inch of space in rooms and corridors and halls was filled with the dense crowd. Only one room was locked, and in that room were the king and queen, the Dauphin and his sister, Thérèse with a few loyal friends. Thérèse was terrified and would have screamed with fright, but the manly little Dauphin watching her, held back his own tears and kept her terror under control by his words and manner, acting with the dignity of a grown-up guardian.

Breathlessly, the little company gathered there listened to the sound of an axe, doors were being battered down, the door of the royal apartment was opened, and an officer of the National Guard knelt before the King, beseeching him to show himself to the frenzied mob. The expression on all faces, the sounds from without were too much for the Dauphin's self-control. He burst into sobs and begged the queen to take him to his room, and while Marie Antoinette was comforting him as best she could, the king went out and stood in the middle of the hall, surrounded by the rabble, speaking in quiet words, of his love for his people. The crowd was delighted at this, but in the meantime, the still greater crowd outside the palace surged through the hall and into the room where the queen and her children were. The National Guards quickly rolled a table up between the queen and the mob, and stood at either side, ready to defend them. Only a table now separated the queen from her enemies, but she was calm and courageous and stood proudly erect with a child on either

LOUIS THE DAUPHIN

side of her, wide-eyed at the sights they saw. Suddenly, the queen trembled with a deathly fear. Before her stood the man whose brawny arm had reached through the paling to grasp the Dauphin. Simon, the cobbler, stood there, hatred and desire for revenge on his face, and Marie Antoinette knew with a quick instinct that this man would bring no good to her child. Then the cries of the Jacobins rent the air and they surged into the room with the fury of wild beasts sure of their prey.

The queen lifted the Dauphin up and set him on a table and whispered to him that he must not grieve or fear or cry, but be a man now, and the child smiled and kissed her hand. Just then a drunken woman flung a red cap—the cap worn by the Jacobins—on the table, and commanded the queen, on pain of death, to put it on.

Calmly, the queen turned to a general standing beside her and told him to place it on her head.

The general, pale with rage at the insult, obeyed in silence and the woman howled with pleasure. But in a moment, the general took the cap off the queen's hair and laid it on the table.

Ever since the King had vetoed the bills, the people had called the King, Monsieur Veto; Marie Antoinette, Madame Veto, and the Dauphin, Little Veto, and now from all sides burst forth the cry, "The red cap for the Dauphin! The tri-colour for little Veto!"

"If you love the nation," cried the woman to the Queen, " put the red cap on your son."

The Queen motioned to one of the ladies to put the red cap on the child, and he, not understanding whether it was a joke or not, stood there in easy grace, as handsome a little prince as ever a nation had.

One of the revolutionary leaders, who had looked

TEN BOYS FROM HISTORY

complacently at the scene, now stood near the queen, and as her eyes met his in calm defiance, he felt a thrill of pity for her and for the little Dauphin, and when he saw the perspiration rolling down the boy's forehead from under the thick woollen cap, he called out roughly:

"Take that cap off the child—don't you see how he sweats?"

The queen's gratified glance thanked him, as she took the cap herself from the Dauphin's head. While this was occurring, the Mayor of Paris had entered the outer hall and was quieting the mob, bidding them disband and leave the palace at once, which they did.

The King sank into a chair, exhausted and agonised, and cried out:

"Where is the queen? Where are the children?" and in a moment the royal victims were together.

The Dauphin's spirits were never long cast down and now he was bubbling over with joy.

"Papa," he cried. "Give me a kiss! I deserve it, for I was truly brave and did not cry or even speak when the people put the red cap on my head."

The king stooped with a dignity which was almost reverent, kissed the boy's broad forehead and pushed back his thick golden hair, then turned to answer a question put by one of the representatives of the people; several of whom were in the room. And all at once these men gathered around the little Dauphin, of whose brilliant mind they had heard so much, and began to question him eagerly on all kinds of subjects, especially about the boundaries of France, and its division into departments and districts, and every question he answered quickly. After each answer he glanced up at his mother inquiringly, and when her face showed that he had answered correctly, his face

LOUIS THE DAUPHIN

beamed with pleasure, and he enjoyed seeing the astonishment on those faces crowding around him. One of those present asked:

"Do you sing, too, Prince?"

The Dauphin glanced again at the queen.

"Mamma," he asked, "shall I sing the prayer I sang this morning?"

Marie Antoinette nodded assent and the Dauphin knelt beside her, and folding his hands and looking up with a sweet look of reverence in his blue eyes, sang in a clear voice:

"Oh heaven, accept the prayer
    I offer here,
Unto his subjects spare
    My father dear."

There was absolute silence in the room, while those faces, before so hard and stern, softened. Then with a single glance at the lovely boy, who was still kneeling, with a look on his face as if in a happy dream, one by one, those revolutionists silently left the room.

But even the prayer and the faith of the Dauphin could not longer save the royal family from their fate.

The people, inflamed to fury by every desire of which the revolutionists could make use, now demanded the dethronement of the King, and the giving of the crown to the Dauphin, in whose name, as he was not yet of age, they intended to govern by means of a committee chosen by themselves. To this the King naturally would not give his consent, and amid scenes and sounds terrible beyond all description, the royal family were declared prisoners of the people, and told that they were to thereafter live in the Temple, which was now the royal prison. As the Tuileries had already been pillaged by the mob, the royal family found themselves without food or clothing, except what they wore. The Dauphin was entirely destitute, but fortunately the Duchess of Sutherland had a small son the age of the Dauphin, and she sent the young prince what he needed in the way of clothing for their departure. On August 13, 1792, the sad procession of royalty left the Tuileries in the late afternoon and were escorted by a great mob of frenzied men and women who acted more like wild beasts than like human beings. At night-fall the carriage reached the Temple and the royal prisoners were taken to that part of the building called "the palace," where they found no comforts or necessities of any kind, and torn sheets even had to be used on the Dauphin's bed. Later while the furies who had the prisoners in their power, were converting the principal tower of the building, not only into a prison, but into the worst one imaginable, the king and his family continued to remain in the palace during the day time, but at night, they were all shut up in the small tower—in four cells whose doors were guarded by soldiers. Two men who had been for years in the service of the king, were allowed to remain with him, and they and their sovereigns passed the time in such occupations as were possible. The King found his principal pleasure in superintending the Dauphin's education, giving him lessons every morning, then at one o'clock if the weather was fine, the royal family would all go into the garden, and the Dauphin would play ball or quoits or run races, as was suitable for his age and activity of body. At two o'clock dinner was served, and afterwards, the Dauphin again had a play hour while the king enjoyed a nap. As soon as he awoke, Cléry, who had been with the Dauphin for several years, would give him writing and arithmetic lessons, and then he would play ball or battledore-and-shuttlecock for awhile,

LOUIS THE DAUPHIN

and then there would be reading aloud until it was time for the Dauphin's supper, after which the king would amuse his children with all sorts of riddles and puzzles and games, and then the Dauphin went to bed.

Little Louis was seven and a half years old when he was first shut up in the Temple, and in those months the king taught him to recite poetry, to draw maps and to make use of arithmetic, but his lessons in arithmetic had to be discontinued because an ignorant guard noticed the multiplication tables that the Prince was learning and reported that he was being taught to speak and write in cipher. One of the king's men was removed from the Temple because it was said that he had used hieroglyphics in order to make secret correspondence between the king and queen easier, and even his explanation that the figures he had made use of were only arithmetic tables which he laid by the Dauphin's bedside every night before retiring, that the young prince might prepare his lesson before breakfast, did not pacify his accusers. So little Louis Charles was taught no more arithmetic, but he continued to learn eagerly all that was offered his quick retentive mind to assimilate. His playfulness and mischievous pranks were a great comfort to the failing spirits of the king and queen, and the tact he showed in his manner and words were nothing less than wonderful in so young a boy. He never mentioned Versailles or the Tuileries or anything which would rouse sad memories in the minds of his parents, but seemed to be constantly on his guard to protect them both from any hints of sorrow which he could prevent.

The royal prisoners were soon removed to the principal tower of the Temple, where the Dauphin occupied a room with the king, until after Louis was taken away for trial, when the Dauphin was placed in his mother's care, and after that time he saw his father only once. The king was condemned to death. Having foreseen it, calmly he had accepted the decree, asking only that he might see his family once to say farewell. This privilege was granted and during the scene which lasted almost two hours, little Louis, born to inherit not glory but misfortune, held his father in his arms and kissed and comforted him in the fashion of a strong man rather than a little child. He did not understand causes, but he saw effects, and he was brave because mamma and papa needed someone beside them, who smiled, and so he held tears back until the time when they were a natural consequence of the final parting with his loved father.

And now little Louis was no longer the Dauphin, but rightful King of France—King of France, only think of it, and scarcely eight years old! Marie Antoinette, from the hour of separation from her husband devoted her entire strength and time to the education of her child, the little King. She felt she had no time to lose, and every moment of the day was made to serve some useful end. Even the games he played had each a purpose. It was a touching sight to see him leaning his elbows on a tiny table, absorbed in reading the history of France, then eagerly telling what he had read, and commenting on it. The queen made a special point of talking to the little King of his royal office, told him of his father's gentleness and mercy to his enemies, and made him promise to be as merciful if he should ever reign, and he soon was made to feel that greatness comes not with titles, but with character, and once in his sleep was heard to murmur:

" I will be good and kind; for I am king." Poor little Louis!

At this time there were wars and rumours of wars out-

LOUIS THE DAUPHIN

side the walls of the Temple. Plots to liberate the queen and her son and to restore little Louis to the throne were set on foot by friends of the royal family, and though one and all failed of execution, they vitally affected the young king's life. When the plots were discovered by which Louis was to be abducted and publicly declared king, the revolutionists became so fearful that the plan might be really carried out, that they decided it was unwise to let him remain with his mother any longer, and the decree went forth that the son of Louis Sixteenth was to be taken from his mother and sister, and given into the care of a tutor to be chosen by the committee representing the people.

The queen was driven almost to madness by this unexpected decree, and when men came to take Louis away from her and carry him to another part of the Tower, she frantically placed herself in front of his bed, and insisted that he should not be taken, but power and force were on the wrong side, and at last, the officers tore the child from his mother's arms and carried him dazed and trembling with fright to his new apartment.

King of France was little Louis in title, but the most lonely, most frightened of all children in the land. For two days and two nights he refused food and held out his arms to his so-called tutor, constantly pleading to be taken back to his mother and sister. And who was his " tutor "? No other than Simon, the cobbler, he whose brawny arms had once stopped the Dauphin's way in the garden of the Tuileries. Simon and his wife had been chosen to guard and care for the little King of France, because they were staunch revolutionists who could be relied on to protect the interests of their party. Historians differ in their accounts of the treatment of the young King by this rough couple, but it seems pretty sure now that during their stay in the Temple they were not altogether cruel to little Louis. He was allowed to play both in his rooms and in the garden, had a billiard table, and a case of mechanical birds for his amusement, and when he grieved for his sister's companionship, another little companion of his own age was found to play with him, and it is also known that during his two sicknesses, Simon and his wife cared for him with as much devotion as if he had been their own child. Whether this was because of the fine salary attached to the position, or from some native kindness underneath his coarse rough exterior, we do not know, but be this as it may, Simon evidently gave only such measure of cruelty to his charge as was insisted on by those who employed him, and it was doubtless, they who forced Simon to do what he did to destroy the child's mental and bodily faculties. Louis was made to share their political opinions, to imitate their coarse manners and even to sing their revolutionary songs, while in place of the mourning he had worn for his father, he now wore the coarsest garments and the red cap of the Jacobins, and was often made to drink and eat far more than was good for him, until at last he was in a condition of body and mind such as his tormentors desired, when he could be made a tool to suit their own ends, because of his weakened and abnormal condition.

No page of history is written in so black an ink nor with so many blots as that on which is recorded the imprisonment and torture of little Louis Seventeenth, the King who never reigned, and no page of history offers a more bewildering puzzle for solution, from the moment of his being taken from his mother's care—a puzzle to which there have been more answers, and about which as much mystery hangs, as about any other incident on the pages of history, and no page has been oftener read and re-read than

LOUIS THE DAUPHIN

this which offers for solution the problem of the ending of this little King who never reigned.

We see him last as a prisoner; thin, haggard, sick unto death, with no sparkle in his lustreless eyes, no motion in his swollen joints, no pretty retort on his lips as of old, and with a sigh we turn from the ghastly sight to the pages of French history where we again read in detail the accounts of his life and death, and then it is for us to decide upon our answer to this riddle which offers more than one solution.

Louis Seventeenth of France, in his ninth year, was imprisoned by the revolutionists and subjected to every kind of torture that a human being could be made to suffer. As a result of that treatment, and of loneliness and cruelty, did he pine and sicken and die a natural death as some accounts say?

Did he, as some say, deliberately resist all the attempts made by his persecutors to enter into conversation with him, by maintaining a complete silence of fifteen months; or had a dumb child been put in his place by friends who had secretly rescued the real little king from his prison, and hidden him in a garret room of the Temple until they could safely liberate him? Then finding the dumb child too healthy to suit their plans, did they, as it is said, replace him by a very sick child, who died in the room where the little king was supposed to be imprisoned, and announce his death to the French nation as that of Louis Seventeenth, the royal prisoner? While the poor little substitute was lying in what was supposedly the coffin of little Louis, had the real King been given a strong dose of opium, and hurriedly placed in the coffin, instead of the substitute, as has been said?

Was the dead substitute carried hastily to the room in

the Tower where the little King had been hidden, while Louis himself, alive and well, was being carried in the coffin to the cemetery? It has been said that the carriage in which the coffin was carried had been especially arranged for this scheme, and that while being driven to the cemetery, Louis was taken from the coffin, and placed in a box under the seat of the carriage, while the coffin was filled with papers that it might not seem too light when the bearers carried it to its final resting-place.

Is it true, do you think, that when the young King awoke from the effects of the drug he had been given, he found himself in a strange place, in a bed in a clear bright room, alone with a faithful woman who knew and loved him? And the plot to rescue him having been immediately discovered, was he hastily sent out of Paris in disguise, while to put his enemies on the wrong trail, another little boy was sent with his parents under the name of Louis, in another direction?

And in spite of the terrible sickness he had, as the consequence of all he had endured, did Louis Seventeenth of France, actually live and escape, to grow up a free citizen in a free country where were neither kings, queens nor tyranny, but liberty, equality and fraternity, not in word but in truth? Who can say positively when so much has been affirmed on all sides of the much argued question?

Difficult, indeed, it is to decide whether little Louis Seventeenth, the Dauphin of France, the king who never reigned, died in the Temple, a victim of the Reign of Terror, or escaped to new lands and a new life.

As we turn the pages of history and read the thrilling story, let each decide for himself the fate of the courageous, charming little sovereign. Each must study out the mystery, and solve the riddle if he can. And whatever one may

LOUIS THE DAUPHIN

read or decide, there in the church of the Madeleine in Paris, may be found this memorial to the little King who never reigned.

IN MEMORY
of
LOUIS XVII
WHO
AFTER HAVING BEHELD HIS ILLUSTRIOUS PARENTS
SWEPT AWAY BY A DEATH
WHICH SORROW REFUSES TO RECOUNT
AND AFTER HAVING DRAINED TO THE VERY DREGS
THE CUP OF ADVERSITY
WAS, WHILE STILL YOUNG
AND ALMOST ON LIFE'S THRESHOLD
CUT DOWN BY THE SCYTHE OF DEATH
HE DIED JUNE VIII—M. DCC. LXXXXV.
HE LIVED X YEARS, II MONTHS & XII DAYS

EDWARD THE BLACK PRINCE
The Boy Warrior

EDWARD THE BLACK PRINCE
The Boy Warrior

MANY of you who have visited Queens College, Oxford, will have seen there, hanging in the gallery above the hall, an old engraving of a quaint vaulted room, where it is said the greatest soldier of his age lived while a student in the college.

This afterwards famous student, who was then about twelve years old was Edward Plantagenet, Prince of Wales, later called the Black Prince. He was also sometimes called the Prince of Woodstock, doubtless, from the fact that he was born in the old palace at Woodstock, in 1330.

He was the son of Edward Third and Queen Philippa, and was one of those rare persons who combine in their characters qualities of both his father and mother. Everyone knows the story of the siege of Calais, when the sternness of King Edward and the gentleness of Queen Philippa were so strikingly shown, and it was the union of those two qualities which gave their son, Edward, that high place which he justly occupies, not only among our English princes, but in the history of all Europe.

He was undoubtedly sent to Queens College, not only because it was the most famous college of that day, but also because it took its name from his mother, Queen Philippa, having been founded by her chaplain.

There, at Queens College, we first see the young prince,

and although six hundred years have gone by since then, many of the customs of to-day were those of young Edward's time as well. The students then were called to dinner by the blast of a trumpet as they are to-day, and then, as now, the Fellows (or post graduates) all sat on one side of the table, with the Head of the college in their midst, in imitation of the pictures of the Last Supper.

The prince must have seen, too, some customs which we know prevailed in his day, but do not see in ours. Thirteen lame, deaf, blind and maimed beggars came each morning into the college hall to receive their portion of food for the day. The porter of the college made his rounds early every morning, to shave the beards and wash the heads of the Fellows, but these and many other quaint customs have perished long ago and still the picture of the Black Prince hangs on the college wall. Tradition tells us that while the proud young prince was receiving such education as befitted his rank in life, a poor boy in the shabbiest of clothes and forgetful of everything except the books and study he loved, was at Queens College too. The characters and lives of John Wycliff, the great reformer, and Edward the Black Prince, were indeed opposite, but it is interesting fo feel that they were educated in the same place, that possibly once in youth, their lives touched, although in later days, one was great in the making of peace and one in the making of war.

The young prince may have been studious, but he also doubtless took advantage of all such diversions as Oxford life offered, and it is natural to picture him in drill and hunt and sports such as were best fitted to his manly vigour, and foreshadowed his enthusiasm in later days for the strenuous game of war.

A mere lad at Queens, we see him first—then a youth,

EDWARD THE BLACK PRINCE

out in the great world watching with keenest interest the doings of courtiers and king, and then we find him a young knight, following the king, his father, in his first great campaign, and a fine young warrior he was both in looks and character, fearless and strong in his black armour which threw into sharp contrast the fairness of his complexion. A brave, handsome young knight was he, Edward Plantagenet, at the time when the English people under King Edward became inspired with a passion for continental dominion.

The Normans had conquered England and now the English were eager to go out and themselves become conquerors, and to further that ambition King Edward and his army set out and ravaged Normandy, pillaging and plundering their way almost to the gates of Paris, and their march was perfectly consistent with the feudal manner of waging war, which was to desolate the country through which they passed, to burn any town that resisted invasion, and to plunder its inhabitants even though they peacefully submitted to the invaders. In this way, King Edward and his army, which included the young Prince Edward and many other noblemen, passed through Normandy, burning and devastating land and property as they went, and they advanced up the left bank of the Seine—their object being, to cross the river at Rouen and then march on to Calais, where they were to be joined by an army of Flemish archers. But their plans received a sudden checkmate.

Philip, the King of France, was at Rouen before them, and had not only encamped on the right bank of the river, but had destroyed the bridges and set guards over all the fords of which the English might make use in crossing.

The English were in a very dangerous position, whether they retreated or went forward. They were separated from the Flemish allies by not only the Seine, but the Somme River, and Philip with his army, which was daily increasing in numbers, was marching towards Calais on the right bank of the Seine, as were Edward and his army on the left bank.

Edward was as firm in his purpose to meet and defeat the enemy, as was Philip in his, and Edward determined to press on at all odds and face and conquer the French forces, and fortune favoured him.

With extreme difficulty, finally, at low tide, he was able to cross the Somme whither Philip was eager to follow, but before Philip's forces were ready to cross the river, the tide had turned, and he was obliged to wait till morning, while Edward now already on the other side of the river, was pressing forward into the country of Ponthieu, which had been part of the marriage portion of his mother, Isabella of France. It was for this special reason, some historians say, that King Edward encamped there, in the forest of Crécy, fifteen miles from Abbeville, saying:

"Let us take here some plot of ground, for we will go no further till we have seen our enemies."

He also added:

"I am on the right heritage of Madam, my mother, which was given her in dowry. I will defend it against my adversary, Philip of Valois."

We do not, of course, know his motives positively, but we may be pretty sure that he would not have been so eager to defend his mother's possessions, had he not felt sure that it would be to his advantage to do so. Accordingly he and his forces encamped in the little village of Crécy, behind which the ground rises into a broad ridge and from here could be seen the surrounding country through which the French army must advance, and the young prince eagerly

EDWARD THE BLACK PRINCE

strained his eyes in search of the advancing enemy, so eager was he to take part in a real battle.

At midnight, when all the army had been cared for and suitably arranged in their tents, King Edward lay down for a much needed rest, but was up again at dawn, when he and the young prince, not only heard mass but also received the sacrament, and we can fancy how that solemn preface to a day which proved so momentous to the Black Prince, must have lingered long in his memory as a sacred recollection.

It was Saturday, the 26th of August, 1346 when King Edward drew his men up in three divisions—one commanded by the prince, assisted by the Earls of Warwick and Oxford, which division consisted of eight hundred men at arms, two thousand archers and one thousand Welshmen. The second division under Lords Arundel and Northampton had only eight hundred men at arms, twelve hundred archers, while the third division, under the king's own command, had seven hundred men at arms and two thousand archers. This division occupied the summit of the hill, from which the king watched the entire battle, never engaging in it—and for this reason.

King Philip was so determined to destroy the English army, that he had hoisted the sacred banner of France, the great scarlet flag, embroidered with the gold lily which was the emblem of France, as a sign that no mercy whatever would be shown to the English, under any conditions. When this Oriflamme, as it was called, was raised, and King Edward saw it, he realised how great the chances of his death would be, should he engage in the battle, and that this would expose, not only the army, but the whole kingdom to the gravest danger, so throughout the entire battle he remained in the tower of a wind-mill on the ridge overlooking the battle-field, while the young prince, who had only been knighted a month before, was practically left in command of the entire army, and went forward into the very heat of the combat.

When the army had been suitably arranged and every earl, baron and knight knew what he was to do in the hour of battle, King Edward mounted his small white horse and rode slowly from line to line among his men, talking earnestly to them of their duty as warriors, and urging them to defend his rights with all their strength. His words and smile were so stimulating that the men were filled with courage as they listened to him, and every man promised to do as the king wished. Then he ordered them all to eat and drink heartily, that they might be thoroughly refreshed in body as well as in spirit and after fulfilling his command, his small army, sat down on the ground at nine o'clock in the morning with their helmets and crossbows beside them, and patiently waited for the attack of an enemy of ten times their number.

Meanwhile, King Philip and his army having crossed the Somme at last, were advancing towards them as fast as possible, and when they were only a short distance from Crécy, King Philip sent four knights ahead of the army, to reconnoitre and bring back news to him of the position and condition of the English forces.

When his knights saw the little army of the English sitting quietly on the ground, calm and courageous, ready to fight when the moment for combat should come—they went back to King Philip and advised him to allow his men who were weary after a long, hard march, to halt and rest over night, so that they might be as well fitted for the battle as the English were. King Philip felt that this was good advice and at once issued the command to halt.

EDWARD THE BLACK PRINCE

The foremost ranks of his horsemen obeyed the order, but the horsemen in the rear pressed forward regardless of the order, determined to have the glory of victory at once, and rode on and on, with fast and furious frenzy until they came in sight of that little army, sitting on the high ridge, waiting for their attack, when they suddenly were filled with apprehension and turned back, throwing all the unmanageable multitude of men behind them into the wildest kind of confusion, but on they charged, their every step watched by the English army, and as the young Prince saw them, in his breast beat the heart of a happy warrior on whose broad young shoulders the burden of his first great responsibility rested lightly. He had been dressed for the battle by the king's own hand, in glistening black armour, with shield and helmet of burnished iron and the horse he rode was as black as his armour, from which he gained the title of the Black Prince, which he was called ever afterwards.

On came the French, with Philip at their head—and his great reliance at this critical moment of attack was on the skill of fifteen thousand archers from Genoa who were his most valued allies. They were extremely tired after their long march on foot, and wished to rest before the attack was made, but seeing the confusion into which his ranks had been thrown, Philip commanded them to give battle at once. They murmured, but were about to comply, when nature unexpectedly conspired to help the English forces.

The sky, a few moments before blue and cloudless, became overcast, a tremendous storm gathered from the west, broke in all its fury of rain, hail and thunder and lightning —even a partial eclipse of the sun occurred. There was a terrible downpour, and to the horror of the moment was added the hoarse cries of crows and ravens which fluttered before the storm, and in the gathering darkness, circled around the heads of the army, terrifying the Italian bowmen who were superstitious, and not accustomed to the severity of Northern storms.

At last the sky cleared, the clouds lifted and the sun shone out again in dazzling brightness, shining directly in the eyes of the Italians, and not only were they blinded by it, but their bows had become so wet by the rain that when they attempted to draw them, they found it impossible.

The sun was shining at the back of the English archers, who could consequently see just where to aim, and as they had kept their bows in cases during the storm, they were perfectly dry, and now the English began to shoot—shot so well and so fast that their arrows poured down like rain on the Genoese, who had never before encountered such archers as these. Unable to stand the storm of shots, they turned and fled ignominiously and from the moment of their flight the panic of the French army was so great that the day was lost.

Seeing the uselessness of the fleeing archers, King Philip was enraged at them and ordered the soldiers to kill them, as they were simply barring the way of his other men to no purpose. So the poor archers were cut down by the swords of their own comrades, and the French horsemen waded through their blood and approached the English.

The confusion among the ranks of the French increased. The old King of Bohemia who was blind, but filled with zeal for the cause, being surrounded by his followers, asked how the battle was progressing. When told the truth he begged to be led forward that he might strike one blow with his sword for the deliverance of France. His followers consented to his wish, but fearing that they

EDWARD THE BLACK PRINCE

might lose him in the press of battle, they tied the reins of their bridles together, with him in their midst, but alas, all were killed together. The crest of the King of Bohemia which consisted of three white ostrich feathers, with the motto Ich dien (I serve) were taken by the Black Prince in memory of that day, and the crest and motto have ever since been used by the Prince of Wales.

During all the time that the battle was raging, King Edward was watching from his hill-top, his glance never for one moment straying from the panorama of the battle-field, as the combat deepened into a mortal one. The French cavalry was close upon the Black Prince. He and his men were in great danger. He was young and inexperienced. The Earl of Northampton hastily sent a messenger to the king, begging him to come down to his son's aid.

King Edward, who had been watching the prince's manœuvres with breathless interest, and had determined on his course in regard to the lad, answered the messenger with a question.

"Is my son killed?"

"No sire, please God," replied the messenger.

"Is he wounded?"

"No, sire."

"Is he thrown to the ground?"

"No, my lord, not so, but he is in the thick of the fray and is in great need of your assistance."

"Return to those who sent you," answered the king, "and tell them not to send for me again while my son is still alive, but to let the youth win his spurs, for I intend if it please God that this day be his."

Such a retort as this showed plainly that King Edward had the greatest confidence in his son's courage and ability and the bold words being repeated to the prince and his men, so raised their spirits that they fought more valiantly than before. Again and again the French army charged on the enemy, but it was of no use. At one moment, the Black Prince was in mortal danger, having been wounded and thrown to the ground, and was only saved by a brave knight, Richard de Beaumont, who was carrying the huge banner of Wales, and who, seeing the prince fall, instantly threw the banner over him as he lay on the ground, and stood on it until he had driven back the enemy, after which the prince was raised up and revived, and took his place again in the battle.

Through all that long summer evening of August 26th, and far into the night, the Black Prince and his army fought the army of France, fought until the flower of the French force lay dead, and their troops were utterly discouraged, and disorganised.

Then seeing that the case was hopeless for them, and that the victory had been won by the sturdy little English army, John of Hainault seized the bridle of King Philip's horse and led him away, led him away from the danger and tumult of the battle-field. Out into the quiet country they rode in silence, with five horsemen only following them. On they journeyed through the blackness of the night and on until they reached Amiens. But of their flight or journey or destination, not one of the victors thought or cared, for the battle-field had become the seat of wild rejoicing and of revelry.

On the field of Crécy great fires were being lighted by tired but jubilant warriors, and torches flamed high to celebrate the victory of the Black Prince and his army over an enemy ten times as strong in numbers. And as the torches flashed and the fire-glow flamed high, King Edward came down from his hill-top and before the whole army, in the red glow of the blazing fires put his arms around the young prince, his son, who had given battle so bravely to the French, and said with solemn earnestness:

"Sweet son, God give you good perseverance. You are my true son, right royally have you acquitted yourself this day, and worthy are you of a crown."

What a moment that was for the young prince!

With the reverence due not only to a king but to his father, for so were sons taught in those chivalrous days, Edward the Black Prince, though hot with the joy of victory, bowed to the ground before his father and gave him all the honour, as his king and commander.

And so ended the great day on which was fought the memorable battle of Crécy, the result of which was not only deliverance of the English army from an imminent danger, but also later the conquest of Calais, which King Edward almost immediately besieged and won, and which remained in the possession of the English from then until the time of Queen Mary.

And from that day, the Black Prince became the idol of the English people, and the terror of the French, who cherished an almost superstitious fear of his youthful valour and strategy in battle, and the king, realising that there was stern stuff in his son, from that day treated him as an equal, and discussed matters of gravest importance with him, as with one in whose counsel he had implicit confidence, and on the day after the battle, they might have been seen arm in arm, walking together on the field of the combat, talking it over in detail, and as they walked, the king asked his son:

"What think you of a battle? Is it an agreeable game?"

What the prince answered we do not know, but we do

TEN BOYS FROM HISTORY

know that in after years whenever he had the game of war to play, he played it in such a masterly manner that his name has come down to us as the most famous warrior of his age. And he won his spurs, remember, at the battle of Crécy, when only a boy of sixteen years!

TYRANT TAD:
The Boy in the White House

Tyrant Tad and Abraham Lincoln

TYRANT TAD:
The Boy in the White House

AT the time when the Civil War was at its height, and Abraham Lincoln, who was then President of the United States, was staggering under an almost crushing load of responsibility, because of his great anxiety for the future of his beloved country, there were many of his enemies, who were bitterly opposed to the continuance of the struggle between the North and the South for the freeing of the slaves, who used to call the good and great president "tyrant" a most unjust word to use in reference to the big-souled, tender-hearted Lincoln.

One day an eminent politician who was leaving the White House, met an acquaintance and in passing him said with a quizzical smile: "I have just had an interview with the tyrant of the White House."

Then noticing his companion's surprise at his making such a speech, he added: *"Tad!"* and passed on, chuckling over his little joke.

And to Tad the title really belonged—to President Lincoln's youngest son—who was a small whirlwind of impetuous despotism; and woe to the man, woman or child who resisted his tempestuous tyranny.

Few did, and the most willing of all his subjects was the great President, whom tyrant Tad ruled despotically.

Before President Lincoln's day there had been a succession of administrations when no children's voices rang through the stately rooms and corridors of the White House, so it was indeed a change when the three Lincoln boys arrived, in March of 1861, bringing with them all the clatter and chatter which belongs to normal healthy boyhood. Robert, who was then eighteen years old only stayed in the White House for his father's inauguration, then went back to Harvard to finish his education, and Willie, and Theodore or " Tad " as he was always called, from his own pronunciation of his name, (the little fellow had a serious defect in his speech which made it hard for him to pronounce words clearly) were left to make the dignified White House echo with their merry laughter and conversations, as they romped through its long passages, careless of the fact that they were on historic ground, as they scattered their balls, bats, kites and other treasures wherever they chose.

They had few playmates, with whom they were allowed to play frequently, except two boys, the sons of a government official, and the four boys' fertile brains were keen to think out all sorts of exciting and mischievous plans which kept their families on the alert to restrain their actions within the bounds of safety and propriety. The boys who were playmates of Tad and Willie were Budd and Hally Taft, and although they were older than the Lincoln boys, they were much like them in temperament and in looks, Budd was fair like Willie Lincoln, and Hally dark, and more like Tad, whose eyes were bright and brown, in keeping with his quick imperious disposition.

One evening in the spring, the four boys were taken to see a minstrel show in the city. They were thrilled by what they heard and saw, and decided on the spot that they

TYRANT TAD

would give a show themselves, and began between the numbers to plan when and where to give it. But, on the following day, when they discussed it again there seemed to be no room suited to their plans either in the White House or at the Taft's, but finally they decided that by having some partitions in the Taft attic, which was roughly divided into small bedrooms, taken down, they could be accommodated. However, fortune favoured the preservation of the Taft home by a sudden shifting of the boys' interest in the direction of the White House. Mrs. Lincoln was called to New York for a week; Willie and Tad had such severe colds and the weather was so rainy, that she wished them to be amused in the house during her absence, and that could only be done by giving them the society of their playmates. Accordingly one day Hally and Budd were thrown into a state of feverish excitement by the arrival of a messenger with Mrs. Lincoln's invitation for them to spend a whole week at the White House.

Besides delivering the invitation, the messenger also asked whether Willie and Tad were there, as they had not been at home since breakfast time, although they had been traced to the Capitol, where they had been seen sitting in the gallery of the House of Representatives, and later treated to lunch in the restaurant of Congress by a gentleman whom the boys always amused, then they had been seen playing marbles with some of the pages in the Capitol, but now where were they? The messenger who was well acquainted with the truants, seemed more amused than alarmed over their disappearance, and soon carried back a note to Mrs. Lincoln accepting the invitation for Budd and Hally, provided the truants should be found! While Budd and Hally were excitedly helping to pack their clothes in a small valise, for the visit, in walked the wanderers. They carried a very large and much dilapidated umbrella which Tad said they had borrowed from the cook—doubtless a Southern mammy who took an endless delight in the boys' pranks, and aided them all she could in their mischievous plans. Tad's pockets were bulging with marbles, which showed how successfully he had played his game with the pages earlier in the day, and both boys had entirely forgotten that they had bad colds. All four soon set out in high glee together, while Tad gave a whoop of joy as they left the house.

"You bet we'll have a good time!" he exclaimed, and from all descriptions of that visit, they certainly must have had it.

On the following day there was a review, and the boys all rode in the President's carriage, looking as severe and dignified as if they had never had a mischievous idea, but, with a feeling of mistrust that such dignity might be only skin deep, a member of the Taft family went to the White House to find out what was going on. To her relief she saw that the building was still standing, but on being ushered in, she noticed that all the orderlies, soldiers and doorkeepers wore broad grins. Asking where the boys were, and being ushered upstairs she came upon Tad, who instantly called out:

"Oh, say, we've got a circus in the attic. We're minstrels. I've got to be blacked up and Willie can't get his dress on—it's too big. Pin it up, will you? Hurry!"

The horrified question, "Does the President know it?" was answered impatiently by Tad.

"Oh, yes, he knows it," said Tad. "He doesn't care. He's got some general or other in there. Come on—hurry!"

Willie was meanwhile struggling with the long,

flowered skirt of a lilac silk reception dress of Mrs. Lincoln's, and Budd was getting into one of her ruffled morning wrappers, while Tad began to sing at the top of his voice:

"Old Abe Lincoln came out of the wilderness——"

"Hush," cautioned Budd, "the President will hear you."

"I don't care if pa does hear, and he don't care either," said Tad. "We're going to sing that in the show." And sing it they did!

Another day when Tad was shouting out a campaign song at the Tafts' about "Old Abe splitting rails," Willie asked Mrs. Taft if she did not think it was disrespectful of Tad to sing such a song. Tad overheard what he said, and kicked a chair, as he always did when displeased, and said:

"Well, everybody in this world knows Pa *did* use to split rails!" But when Mrs. Taft explained to him why she thought he ought not to say or sing this, Tad said with equal decision:

"Well, I'll sing John Brown's body then." However headstrong he seemed, he was really very affectionate, and willing to be convinced that he was wrong, if any one approached him in the right way.

There was much to occupy the boys' attention in Washington, and they were especially interested in the models of locomotives and steamboats in the Patent Office, where they spent much time, and they were also sometimes to be found making a survey of the White House grounds under the guidance of a good-natured engineer. At other times they invaded the McClellans' house, where they were allowed to play with the baby and where General and Mrs. McClellan were very kind to them, and of course they never missed a review, even riding in the staff, when the bridle of Willie's horse was held by the Duc de Chartres and Budd's by the Comte de Paris, while Hally and Tad rode in front of the aides, sitting as erect and stiff as if they were the chief features in the parade.

On another day, Tad was not allowed to go to the review, as he had not been well the day before. The review took place across the Long Bridge, and after the President's carriage had passed down the line, a rickety cart came clattering by, drawn by a shambling old horse, and driven by a grinning negro boy. In it were Tad, Willie, Budd and Hally in new Zouave uniforms, their swords at a salute! Many a soldier sighed and smiled as that cart passed by, but there was never a smile on the faces of the Zouaves, who had paid the darkey a quarter from their precious circus money to drive that load of glory!

Having the uniform ready they formed themselves into a military company called " Mrs. Lincoln's Zouaves." Much amused by their military enthusiasm she presented them with a flag, and the President formally reviewed them. Willie was colonel, Budd, major, and Hally, captain, while Tad insisted on having the rank of drum-major or nothing, and all of them had old-fashioned swords which were given to them by General McClellan, who greatly enjoyed their pranks and sometimes suggested new ones. When other amusements failed, the quartet spent their time on the flat roof of the White House, which was perfectly safe, being surrounded by a strong balustrade. There they built a cabin, and the roof was in turn a quarter-deck, or a fort, and they used to raise and lower the flag with proper ceremony, and look off through a spy-glass for a " strange sail," and Budd's sister tells how one day when she ascended to the stronghold with a stern demand for her

TYRANT TAD

scissors, which had been missing for several days she was received at the "side" with such strict naval etiquette that she meekly retreated without the scissors.

That first year when President Lincoln was in office was a happy one for his boys and their companions, but all too soon the pleasures came to an end, for Willie Lincoln was stricken with typhoid fever, of which he died. Then the Tafts left Washington and moved to the north, so of the merry group of boys, "Tad" alone remained to enliven the White House, and to amuse himself as best he could in the long days which seemed so quiet in comparison to those which he and his companions had spent together.

But Tad, who was now ten years old, was equal to any emergency, and as resourceful as a dozen ordinary boys, and after the first bitter loneliness had worn off, he made as much commotion by himself as all four boys had made together, and soon became an object of popular attention, as he galloped madly around the grounds on his pony, driving him at break-neck speed, or training his team of dogs on the lawn, or urging his goats to do some impossible feat.

One of the stories told about him at that time was that on a certain day a party of dignified ladies were solemnly and with due reverence inspecting the famous East room, when they heard a deafening clatter at the end of the corridor where the Lincolns' private apartments were, then came a shout of "Get out of the way there!" and Tad the irrepressible, galloped into the room driving a tandem team of goats harnessed to a chair! Up the room and down again and out of the front entrance went the goats and Tad like a flash of lightning, leaving the ladies aghast at a spectacle to which they had found no reference in their guide books.

To his mother's great distress, an interested but not

over-thoughtful friend, gave Tad a tool chest, which of course delighted him, and which at once suggested to him the idea of opening a cabinet shop to manufacture furniture for hospital use, but he fortunately discovered an old wagon to experiment on, and forgot the shop; turning his attention also to any and every object which he could bore, chisel, saw or hack with his tools. Nothing was said in remonstrance until he began to experiment on the old-fashioned mahogany furniture in the East room, when that tool chest mysteriously disappeared and no amount of searching ever brought it to light again.

As he was unable to exist without some new outlet for his feelings he decided to have a theatre and give shows, for which purpose he appropriated an unused room in the White House, and had a fine time fitting it up with a stage, seats, orchestra, drop-curtain and all. At that time, Mr. Carpenter, an artist, was at work on a portrait of President Lincoln and his Cabinet, and when it was found necessary to take several photographs of the room in the White House which was to be the background for the painting, Tad's theatre was offered to the photographers to use in developing their pictures, and Mr. Carpenter used to tell with a chuckle of delight how all went well till Tad suddenly discovered the invasion of his room, when he fell upon the artist and blamed him in a fiery burst of temper, for letting the men into his room, and then went up and calmly locked the door, pocketed the key and walked off, leaving the astonished photographers without occupation, as their apparatus and chemicals were in the room. But that made no difference to tyrant Tad—no one should go into his theatre, he said, and no amount of urging moved him. Finally the President was asked to deal with the young rebel, as was usual when Tad's behaviour pre-

TYRANT TAD

sented impossibilities to the general public. Mr. Lincoln was sitting ready to be photographed at the time. He listened quietly to the story, and then called Tad and told him to go and open the door. Tad rushed off, muttering and shaking his head but he absolutely refused to obey, even though Mr. Carpenter made use of all the arguments he could think of, to make him yield. Reluctantly the artist went back to the room where the President sat and he at once asked:

"Has the boy opened that door?"

Mr. Carpenter was obliged to say that he had not, and Lincoln slowly rose, compressing his lips and strode out of the room. Soon he returned, carrying the key, which he handed to the artist saying apologetically:

"He is a peculiar child. He was violently excited when I went to him. I said 'Tad, do you know you are making your father a great deal of trouble?' He burst into tears and at once gave me the key."

This little incident shows the affectionate side of tyrant Tad who could always be led, but never driven, and it was to his father's gentle diplomacy that the fiery, impulsive little fellow always responded.

Often Tad would perch on his father's knee, or even on his shoulder, while weighty conferences were going on, and sometimes would insist on spending a whole evening in the executive mansion, finally falling asleep on the floor, when the President would tenderly pick him up and carry him off to bed.

At other times, with affairs of the gravest importance awaiting his consideration, President Lincoln would sit with his arms around the boy, telling him anecdotes and stories of which he had an endless fund, until the boy's drowsy eyes closed, when President Lincoln would gently carry him to his room, and then go back to ponder on weighty matters of national importance far into the night, but never retiring for the night without a last look at the little fellow who was the supreme joy and comfort of his life.

He was very fond of animals, and for a long while goats were his special favourites, during which time a large and flourishing family of them decorated the lawns and roads about the White House, and that the goats were very important members of the family is shown by the fact that at a time when Mrs. Lincoln and Tad had gone away for a week and the family were living at the Soldiers' Home, Lincoln wrote to his wife: "Tell dear Tad that poor Nanny Goat is lost and we are in distress about it. The day you left, Nanny was found resting herself and chewing her little cud on the middle of Tad's bed, but now she's gone! The gardener kept complaining that she spoilt the flowers, till it was decided to bring her down to the White House, which was done, but on the second day she disappeared and has not been heard of since."

Tad was evidently consoled for this tragic event by not one goat, but a whole family of them, for about a year later Mr. Lincoln ended a business telegram to his wife in New York with the words: "Tell Tad the goats and father are very well," and with a gleam of that humour for which he was famous, the great-hearted, patient man added, "especially the goats!"

Again a friend of the Lincolns' sent them a fine live turkey to be used for the President's Christmas dinner, but long before that time the turkey and Tad had become bosom friends. Tad named him Jack and used more patience in trying to teach him tricks than he could ever be persuaded to give to his lessons. One day just before the

TYRANT TAD

holiday, while President Lincoln was discussing a matter of gravest importance with his cabinet ministers, Tad burst into the room as if shot out of a cannon and sobbing as if nothing could ever comfort him. Of course, business came to a standstill while Tad explained; Jack was about to be killed, he must not be killed, it was wicked, and Tad had forced the executioners to stay their hands while he laid the case before the President. Jack should *not* be killed! sobbed out the indignant little tryant.

"But," said the President quietly, "Jack was sent to be killed and eaten for this very Christmas."

"I can't help it," roared Tad, between his sobs. "He's a good turkey and I don't want him killed."

The President of the United States paused in the midst of the important business under discussion, and with the gravity due to a solemn occasion, took a card and wrote on it an order of reprieve for the turkey, which Tad seized, and fled with all speed, and Jack's life was saved. He became very tame, and roamed peacefully about the grounds at will, enduring petting and teasing alternately, from his capricious young master. At that time the White House was guarded by a company of soldiers from Pennsylvania with whom the turkey was a great favourite. The tents of these soldiers were on the Potomac side of the White House, at the end of the South lawn, and in the summer of 1864 a commission was sent down from Pennsylvania to take the votes of the Pennsylvania soldiers in Washington for the coming election. Tad was, as usual, much interested in what was going on, and dragged his father to the window to see the soldiers voting, while Jack stalked around among them, apparently intelligent and interested.

"Does Jack vote?" asked Lincoln with a roguish twinkle in his eye.

For a moment Tad was nonplussed by the unexpected question, but he was as quick as he was keen, and rallying, he answered:

"Why no, of course not. He isn't of age yet!"

Another of Tad's great diversions was to stand around among the crowd of office-seekers who daily filled the corridors leading to President Lincoln's office, for their turn to see the President. Tad used to talk with them, while they waited, asking them all sorts of impertinent questions which were always taken in good faith, because he was the President's son, and known to be such a favourite that he might be a valuable ally. Some of the office-seekers came day after day without ever obtaining an interview with Lincoln, and with these Tad grew quite intimate; some of them he shrewdly advised to go home and chop wood for a living, others he tried to dismiss by promising them that he would speak to his father of their case, if they would not come back again unless they were sent for, and with one and all he was a great favourite, he was so bright and cunning, and too, all were eager to have the good will of the little fellow, for motives not always the highest. This, shrewd little Tad discovered, and he decided to put his popularity to use, so one morning when the line of callers began to form, they found Tad standing at the foot of the staircase, where he made every one who passed up pay him five cents for the benefit of the Sanitary Fund, as he explained while he was gathering in the nickels.

This enterprise was so satisfactory that he decided to give one of the Sanitary Commission Fairs which were then being held all over the country, and placing a table in the entrance hall of the White House he stocked it with all the odds and ends which his amused friends could be made to contribute, as well as with some food begged from the pan-

TYRANT TAD

try, and some of his own broken toys. One can well imagine the difficulty of getting in or out of the White House that day with any change in one's pocket, and when night came Tad's accounts made him chuckle with delight, and decide on a still bolder enterprise. This required capital, however, but that did not daunt him, for he had quite an amount of pocket money saved up, and with it he bought out the entire stock of an old woman who sold gingerbread and apples near the Treasury Building, wheedled a pair of trestles and a board from a carpenter, and set up shop in the very shadow of the stately portico of the White House, to the horror of some who saw the performance, and to the intense amusement of others who were always watching to see what Tad would do next.

As long as his stock lasted, he did a heavy business, for it was an excellent chance for those who wished to buy his favour, to do so, and his pockets were well lined with bills when he shut up shop that night, but being as generous as he was shrewd, capital and profit were soon squandered, and it is said the little merchant went penniless to bed.

In vain were all attempts to make Tad study. He never had any time for such dull things as books, when there was all out-of-doors for his restless self to rove in, and his father did not seem grieved or worried when tutors came and went, shaking their heads over a boy who was such a whirlwind of activity that they had no chance to become acquainted with him, although he was keener than they, and weighed them each in the balance and found them wanting before any one of them had been with him twenty-four hours.

When appealed to in regard to the matter, the President would say:

"Let him run. There's time enough yet for him to

learn his letters and get poky." And so the boy followed out his own impetuous desires, and although so backward in regard to books, he understood far more about mechanics and trade than other boys of his own age, and for all his impetuosity and despotism, he had a very tender conscience and a loving nature. A friend of Lincoln's tells of sitting with the President once when Tad tore into the room in search of some lost treasure, and having found it, flung himself on his father like a small whirlwind, gave him a wild fierce hug, and without a word, or even giving his father time to do or say anything, rushed out as impetuously as he had come in. It is needless to say that he was no respecter of persons, young Tyrant Tad; he knew no law, he had no restraint that barred him from any part of the house at any time, but came and went, and did and said whatever pleased his vagrant fancy. Not unfrequently while the President was occupied with his cabinet, Tad would burst into the room bubbling over with some personal grievance which demanded immediate attention or with some pathetic story about a shabbily dressed caller who was being sent away by the ushers, to Tad's great anger. At other times he would become deeply interested in some young person who had come to the President with a request which Tad had heard first himself, and insist on dragging him into the President's presence at once to tell the story, and make his request, and so thoroughly was the President in sympathy with this tender-hearted trait of his son, that he always received such protégés of Tad's with interest and helped them if he could.

Tad had his likes and dislikes, and took no pains to conceal them, and one morning when he broke in on his father's privacy and found with him a Cabinet officer for whom he had no liking, he cried out:

TYRANT TAD

"Why are you here so early? What do *you* want?" probably to the chagrin of his father, who doubtless talked with him seriously later in the day about showing such discourtesy to an elder.

Quick to take up a new interest, and as quick to throw it aside, one day when the Secretary of War, Mr. Stanton, found Tad fussing around his office, Mr. Stanton, just for the fun of it, commissioned Tad a lieutenant of the United States Volunteers; this excited Tad so greatly that he hurried off and on his own responsibility ordered a quantity of muskets sent up to the White House at once, and then gathered together the house-servants and gardeners, and organised them into a company, drilled them for service, and then actually dismissed the regular sentries on the premises, and ordered his new recruits on duty as guards. Robert Lincoln, who was then at home, having discovered Tad's scheme, thought that the men who had been at work all day, ought to be free at night, and told Tad so, but Tad would not listen to him, so Robert appealed the case to his father, who only laughed, as he generally did at Tad's pranks, thought the whole thing a good joke, and gave no orders to the refractory young lieutenant. Tad, however, soon grew tired of being on watch himself, and went to bed, when his recruits were quietly relieved from duty, and there was no guard over the President's house that night.

While he sported his commission as lieutenant Tad looked the part, having from some source got a uniform suitable for the occasion, and in that proud costume he had himself photographed to the great delight of his admiring circle of friends.

Tad's tenth birthday was celebrated by a visit which he made with his father and a party of friends to the Army of the Potomac, which was then encamped on the banks of the Rappahannock, opposite Fredericksburg, the visit being made because the President thought a glimpse of the Nation's Chief Executive might put fresh courage into the weary soldiers. The visit was five days long and a more restless member of a party than Tad was, cannot be imagined. By the end of the first day he had exhausted all the resources of the encampment, and begged to go home, but there were any number of reviews and parades for which the President was obliged to stay, and these somewhat diverted Tad, for a handsome young soldier was detailed as the boy's special escort, and a little grey horse consoled him partially for the beloved pony left at home. It is said that those reviews and the part Tad played in them will never be forgotten by the men who saw or took part in them, and this is the way they have been described.

"Over hill and dale dashed the general-in-chief with his company of officers in gay uniforms, sparkling with gold lace, and escorted by the Philadelphia Lancers, a showy troop of soldiers. At their head, seen afar, rose the tall form of Lincoln, conspicuous always by his great height and lean awkward figure, and as they passed, ever on the flanks of the hurrying column flew, like a flag or a small banner, Tad's little grey riding coat. His short legs stuck out straight from his saddle, and sometimes there was danger that he would be shot out of his seat at some sharp turn in the road, but much to the astonishment of everybody, the hard-riding reckless youngster turned up at headquarters safe and sound every night, exhausted but flushed with the excitement of the day. Everywhere they went on horseback he divided the honours with his father, and whenever the soldiers saw the tall figure of their much loved President, and fresh-faced merry Tad, they cheered themselves

TYRANT TAD

hoarse, but in response to the cheers Tad firmly refused to salute as he was told to do, saying:

"That's the way General Hooker and father do, but I am only a boy," and paid no attention to the notice he attracted.

Even with the excitement of the reviews, so restless was Tad during those days with the army of the Potomac, and so steadily did he plead with his father to go home, that finally to quiet him, the President said:

"Tad, I'll make a bargain with you. If you will agree not to say anything more about going home until we are ready to go, I will give you that dollar you want so badly."

The teller of that story who was on the spot at the time, says, that although having a great desire for the dollar, Tad did murmur a few times after this, and when they were ready to go back to Washington, Lincoln held up a dollar bill before Tad, asking:

"Now, Taddie, my son, do you think you have earned this?"

Tad hung his head and said nothing, but the President handed it to him, saying:

"Well, my son, although I don't think you have kept your part of the bargain, I will keep mine, and you cannot reproach *me* with breaking faith, anyway!" Tad's face showed that he understood the value of that greenback, as well as his father's reproof.

The long terrible months of the War of Secession wore slowly away, now illuminated by the joy of a victory, now overshadowed by the gloom of defeat, and meanwhile President Lincoln was criticised by friends and foes, alike by those who did not understand, and by those who would not appreciate the vastness of the ideal underlying the pain and tragedy of the war. But the President struggled on, wearing out his heart and his strength, but his courage and his faith never failed, and through all the suspense and responsibility of those years, Abraham Lincoln stood firm, Captain of the Ship of State, steering her safely into the desired haven.

The war came to an end. The armies of the Union had crushed out the great rebellion. Peace came to the troubled land, and Lincoln felt that he had fulfilled his mission,—that he could now enjoy in unclouded happiness that second term on which he was just entering.

At that time, when though men were jubilant over the end of the great struggle, there was still in some hearts a revengeful spirit towards the conquered, and when in one of his speeches Lincoln asked:

"What shall we do with the rebels?"

A man in the audience cried:

"Hang them!"

The President's elbow received a violent jerk and Lincoln looked hastily down before replying. As usual Tad was close beside his father, and had taken the only means of attracting his attention:

"No, father," he said, "don't hang them—hang on to them!"

"Tad's got it," said Mr. Lincoln, beaming with pleasure at the little fellow's idea. "He's right, we'll hang on to them!"—and that remark of Tad's with the response it brought out, has become one of the most famous memories of Tad.

In another historic scene we find him figuring. It was the night of President Lincoln's last long speech, that of April 11, 1865. News had just come of the fall of Richmond and Petersburg, and the White House was a blaze of

TYRANT TAD

lights from attic to cellar, in honour of the occasion, while all over the country a wave of joy swept, for now it was felt that the end of the long struggle was in sight. A great crowd of people had gathered outside the White House and the sound of their cheers and shouts was like the roar of the ocean, and the clamour of brass bands and the explosion of fireworks, added to the general confusion and noise.

Inside the White House, the President and some friends sat long at dinner, after which the President would be expected to make a speech to the expectant crowd, but he lingered at the table, as though loath to end its pleasant intercourse, while Tad grew impatient at such a long period of inaction, and crept away. Soon he was discovered at a front window, out of which he was frantically waving a Confederate flag, which someone had given him. The impatient crowd outside, eagerly watching for something to happen, when they saw the little figure with the big rebel flag, applauded uproariously, for Tad and his pranks were one of the features of the White House. But when the dignified old family butler discovered the youngster he was horrified. After a long struggle with him which delighted the crowd, Tad was captured and dragged in, and his flag confiscated while the old servant exclaimed:

"Oh, Master Tad, the likes of it, the likes of a rebel flag out of the windows of the White House.—Oh, did I ever!"

Struggling out of his conqueror's clutches, Tad rushed tempestuously to his father to complain about such treatment, but Mr. Lincoln, having finished dinner, had just stepped into a centre window, from which he could look out on the great crowd of people below him, and was waiting for the mighty cheer that welcomed him to die away. Then he spoke, and as the first words:

"We meet to-night, not in sorrow, but in gladness of heart,"—fell on the ears of the throng, a mighty hush enveloped the surging mass of human beings whom he was addressing.

His speech was written on loose sheets of paper, which as he finished, fluttered one by one from his hand to the ground. The candle which should have given him light, was not where he could see to read by it, so he took it from its place, and held it in one hand, while he continued with his reading, and still the pages fluttered to the ground one by one.

Tad, meanwhile, finding his father occupied, had seized the chance of despoiling the forsaken dinner table of all the dainties still on it, but after this diversion began to pall, he looked about for some new excitement. Hearing the President's voice addressing the crowd, Tad crept behind his father, and amused himself by picking up the fluttering pages as they fell. The President was reading slowly and the pages dropped too seldom to suit impatient Tad.

"Come, give me another!" he whispered loudly, pulling the leg of his father's trousers. The President made a little motion of his foot towards Tad, but gave no other sign that he heard the whispered command, and continued to voice his grave and wise thoughts on Reconstruction.

Below was that vast sea of upturned faces—every eye fixed on the face of the much loved President. At the window, his face radiant with patriotic joy stood Abraham Lincoln—that heroic figure, reading the speech which was to be his last word to the people.

Beside him, creeping back and forth on his hands and

knees after the fluttering pages, and sometimes lifting an eager face to his father, was Tad, the boy of the White House, and there let us leave him, close beside that father to whom he was both comfort and joy, through dark years of storm and stress. Let us leave Abraham Lincoln, and Tad, his cherished son, together there in the sight of the people to whom they were so dear, before the black curtain of sorrow falls over them, that Tad's merry face may linger in our memory untouched by the sorrow of a nation's tragedy.

HUGH OF LINCOLN:
The Boy Chorister

HUGH OF LINCOLN:
The Boy Chorister

IN the old Cathedral town of Lincoln, in England, there lived a widow named Beatrice, whose other name we do not know, we only know that she had a son named Hugh, dearer to her than anything on earth, who was now old enough to go to the little school kept by two elderly dames at the other end of town from that in which Beatrice and Hugh lived. Beatrice was full of fear lest Hugh should come to harm in passing through that quarter of the city in which a great number of Jews lived, while on his way to and from school. But her neighbours laughed at these fears, telling her that she would make a weakling and a girl of Hugh, and so reluctantly she parted with him daily, and watched him as he walked gaily off with his companions.

Hugh was a bright, affectionate little fellow with merry blue eyes, and a clear, high soprano voice, and could carry a tune so correctly and sing so sweetly that he was called "the little chorister," and often as he walked through the streets, the notes of his song would ring out, carried far away by the wafting breezes, and many a person anticipated hearing that song as its singer passed by.

Beatrice had brought Hugh up with a deep feeling of religious devotion for Christ and his holy Mother, and his favourite song was "O loving Mother of the Redeemer," which he had heard the other older boys singing at school, and taught himself, verse by verse, until he could sing them all. Then as he walked to school each day the words rang out clear and distinct in the childish voice, rang in Jewish ears to which the sound of Christian praise was torture, and the Jews began to wonder how a lad who offended their ears with such anthems could be made to sing no more, for in those days there was much warfare among Jews and Christians, and there was a bitter prejudice against the Jews, who were popularly, and often unjustly accused of committing cruel acts of various kinds. And it is said, how truly we do not know, that a Jew whose name was Copin, in whose heart there lurked all kinds of brutish instincts, solved the problem of silencing Hugh's song in this way:

Calling together a number of his friends, he reminded them of their ancient custom of imprisoning a Christian and crucifying him in mockery of that Christ whom he professed to serve, and suggested that the boy who sang his hymn with such triumphant joy, should be the victim of their custom.

The idea met with the hearty approval of the other Jews, and plans were made at once to carry it out. Accordingly, when next the little Chorister passed through the street singing his favourite song, a man's smiling face looked into his, and a deep voice questioned him about his song, and as to where he learned such beautiful words. The interest was so genuinely expressed that little Hugh was most responsive, saying:

"My mother and the dames at school, sir, have taught me all I know about the Holy Virgin and the art of song. The Holy Mother loves and protects her children when they sing such hymns, and so I love to sing as you have heard me,

HUGH OF LINCOLN

sir, and at this school I learned the words which speak the Virgin's praise."

Copin, the Jew, looking into the boy's fair, flushed face, felt a pang of remorse, cut like a knife. Could he do it? Then hardening his heart he thrust from him all instincts of mercy, and with a forced smile asked:

"And will you enter my house, my boy, and sing your song to her who is my mother, and who can no longer go out to hear sweet singers, because of her infirmity—it will be a breath of air from heaven if you can spare the time."

Forgetful of his mother's caution to enter no strange house without permission, eager to sing his song to a new listener, the lad followed his smiling host, and there within the gate, within the door, he found no aged mother to comfort with his song—no longer was the Jew a smiling host. Fierce, black and strong, he turned on Hugh and spoke in words as clear as those of Hugh's own song.

"We want no words of Christ and now we will crucify you that you may be with him you worship so. Now may the Holy Virgin comfort you."

Like one who walks in dreams was Hugh led up to a large dark room where he was told that he must stay.

"Alone? Will you not tell my mother? Oh, sir, she will be dead from fright unless I come from school! I disobeyed her, sir, in coming here, and I must go to her now."

A harsh, cruel laugh was his answer.

"Let your Holy Mother see to that," said the Jew's taunting voice. "She can work miracles, you say, let her get you out of here and calm your mother's fears."

For ten days, long days of agony and fear, Hugh stayed within that room, and all that time his mother's days and nights were full of agony, as hot with frenzy through the town she roamed, crying aloud for Hugh. Neighbours and friends assisted in the search and town officials helped in every way they could, but there were no tidings of the boy. Almost mad with misery, Beatrice sat in her room, looking with a fixed stare at its four walls, when a soft knock roused her. A boy was there, the playfellow of Hugh.

"What have you come to tell me? Have you news of him?" she gasped.

The boy nodded. "We went home from school with him that day," he said, "but left him at the corner where the 'Jewry' begins, and looking back I saw him talking to a man beside the gate——"

"And can you show me where that was?" The boy nodded again, and Beatrice grasped his hand as in a vise. "Take me there," she said, "why did you wait so long?"

"I was at grandfather's, visiting," he said. "I never knew that Hugh was gone till I came back to-day."

While he was talking, they were hurrying down the stairs and through the streets and into the Jewish part of town. Before a large stone house, they paused. "It was here," her companion said and Beatrice dropped his hand. "I have no further need of you," she said. "This is no place for you, leave me to find my boy, but pray, lad, pray the Holy Virgin that he be not dead."

There is no instinct half so keen as mother's love when aroused. Beatrice forced an entrance into that house where Hugh had been imprisoned, searched it through from roof to cellar, but found no trace of him for whom she looked. Then, mad with disappointment, she rushed from the house and to its rear. Hark! She listened, wild-eyed,—the song—the song—"O loving Mother of the Redeemer." Whence came it? The words rang clear! With the strength of man or ox, she lifted the heavy stone above an ancient well

HUGH OF LINCOLN

whose waters were dried. There, upright in the narrow cut, was he for whom she searched, but now beyond recall of love or longing.

"Hugh!" her piercing cry rang out, rang out like a challenge to her dead to rise, for still came clear and sweet the song:

"O loving Mother of the Redeemer!"

Though he no longer was alive, the little Chorister was singing as of old. So loud, so clear, so sweet the words of his song rang out, that in the street a crowd began to gather, and when they saw the well and heard the song, each one was filled with awe and fear of this great miracle, and someone ran to fetch a priest, who came in haste to see the child, who, though dead, yet sang his song of praise.

Copin, the Jew, outwitted by a mother's instinct, was captured within that very house where he had imprisoned Hugh, and when they dragged him forth and made him stand beside the opened well and listen to that miraculous song, beads of agony stood on his forehead, a passion of remorse possessed him, and he confessed his ghastly deed and how he did it; and shivering with fear, for men were far more superstitious in those days, than they are now in this prosaic age—Copin confessed with ill-concealed awe, how when they tried to bury the little Chorister, the earth could not be made to cover his fair form, that when they tried to sink it under water, it could only be made to float, and that then in desperation it had been thrown into the pit.

A fury of rage possessed the crowd gathered around the Jew while he told his hideous tale, with a wild cry of revenge they fell upon him—caused him to be dragged through the streets of Lincoln by wild horses, and then hanged him, by order of the King.

Meanwhile, with tender reverence, the boy whose love

for the Holy Mother was so great that even death itself could not hush his praise of her, was lifted from the dark, damp pit, and gently laid upon a bier, which was then carried in hushed silence to the vast Cathedral followed by a great throng of followers.

"O holy Mother of the Redeemer!"—the words were wafted on the still air as they had been in days when Hugh walked through the streets, and heads were all uncovered, the hum of voices stilled—as the young chorister was carried by.

Poor Beatrice! she followed without knowing where she went—and Hugh! Hugh! was her piteous cry, until in momentary respite, she fainted by the bier when it at last was laid before the altar in the dim Cathedral nave.

"O loving Mother of the Redeemer!" the words still rang out clear and sweet. A monk who was at hand, spoke thus to the miraculous dead, in awe-struck voice:

"Oh, dear child, I beg thee in the name of the Holy Trinity, tell me why thou singest even now?"

And clear and distinct rang out the words of Hugh:

"In truth I should have become silent long since, but Jesus Christ decrees that his power and glory be kept in mind, and for the worship of his Mother dear, yet may I sing 'O loving Mother' loud and clear. This source of mercy, Christ's sweet Mother, I always loved and served as well as I knew how, and when the time came for me to yield up my life, she came to me, and bade me sing this anthem even in dying, and as I sang it seemed as if she laid a grain upon my tongue, and said to me, 'My little child, I will take thee to myself when the grain is taken from thy tongue. Be not afraid, I never will forsake thee.'"

With quick impulse the holy monk reached forward, and took from Hugh's tongue the grain. Ah! the song

HUGH OF LINCOLN

grows softer—softer—dies away. The sweet voice is stilled for ever. The Holy Mother has taken the little Chorister unto herself.

The monk, at this, fell prostrate on the ground and wept, oh, bitterly, and as he lay there weeping, a woman blind for years, crept up beside the bier, touching the child's cold forehead with a loving hand.

"I SEE!" her cry startled through the arches of that vast Cathedral! "I see—I am no longer blind! He is a saint, this little Chorister. Praise be to Jesus Christ and to his Mother dear!"

This miracle and many others of its kind did Hugh of Lincoln, lying on his bier, so it is said by ancient chroniclers, and so was Hugh, the little Chorister, sainted in life and so called in his death.

DAVID FARRAGUT:
The Boy Midshipman

David Farragut

DAVID FARRAGUT
The Boy Midshipman

IT was a day in late October, in the year 1812. Down the Delaware River, came slowly sailing the frigate *Essex,* which was one of a fleet being sent to cruise along the Atlantic coast for the protection of American vessels from their English enemies, for 1812 was the year when the war between England and America was declared, and for this reason.

England had for a long time been at war with France. Any vessel going to or from a French port was liable to be attacked by an English man-of-war, and the English government even claimed the right to search American vessels to see whether any English sailors were on board. And worse than that, many American sailors were accusèd, and falsely, of being English deserters and were taken from their own vessels and forced to serve on English ships. All attempts of America to adjust this matter peacefully were refused, and in 1812 America was obliged to declare war against Great Britain, and in consequence a squadron was fitted out to cruise along the Atlantic coast, to protect American vessels from the English.

The *Essex* was in command of Captain Porter, and as she was not ready to start when the rest of the fleet did, she sailed alone down the river through the quiet bay, and out into the ocean, and as she sailed, she bore little resemblance to our war vessels of to-day, so clumsily fashioned

TEN BOYS FROM HISTORY

was she, being made of wood, with only one covered deck, and the open forecastle and quarter-deck above it, and had but two tiers of guns—the largest frigate carried sixty guns, besides a large pivot gun at the bow, and were noted for their speed, though in comparison to modern warships they were as a tortoise is to a hare.

Down the river sailed the *Essex* to join the sister-vessels of her fleet, with a pennant flying from her mast-head, on which were the words, *"Free trade, and sailors' rights,"* for both of which, Captain Porter was ready to fight.

On the deck of the *Essex* as she swung slowly out to sea, stood Captain Porter, and by his side stood the proudest boy in all America that day, David Farragut, a little midshipman in a shining uniform which boasted more brass buttons than the years of its wearer's life—for David was only ten years old, and this is how he came to be in such an important position on that October day.

Born on a farm near Knoxville, Tenn., on the fifth of July, in 1801, David Glascow Farragut had a rich inheritance of courage and energy, both from his mother and father—one being a Spaniard who had come to America during the Revolutionary war, through his desire to help the Colonists in their struggle for liberty, the other a brave, energetic young Scotch woman.

The little farm was miles away from any other dwelling place, and around it there was only a wilderness of forest trees, so that little David and his brother were not allowed to go out of sight of the house, because of the wild animals prowling through the woods and the Indians who often lurked near. One day while the father was away hunting, the Indians came and tried to force their way into the house, but brave Elizabeth Farragut was too quick for them, with

FARRAGUT

fierce courage she guarded the entrance to the house—axe in hand—first sending the boys up to a loft under the roof, where they crouched in silence for hours, while the courageous mother kept the Indians at bay, and finally they tired of their fruitless attempt and went away.

When David was seven years old his father was appointed sailing master in the navy, and in consequence the family moved to the plantation on the bank of Lake Pontchartrain near New Orleans, where the father's headquarters were to be. As he was devoted to his children, he generally kept them with him when he was off duty, and many times took them out in his little sail boat on the lake in the fiercest kind of storms, storms so severe that sometimes they could not even get home, but would spend the night on an island, warmly wrapped in a heavy sail, or tucked up under a protecting coverlet of sand. When he was blamed for this, he always answered:

"Now is the time to conquer their fears," and continued to take his boys on such excursions as before.

One day while George Farragut was out on the lake fishing, he saw an old man in a boat alone and evidently sick.

Pulling alongside of him, Farragut found him unconscious, and towing his boat to shore, carried him to the house, where Elizabeth Farragut nursed him with as tender care as if he had been her father. His disease was yellow fever, and in five days he died, and brave Elizabeth Farragut survived him by only a few days, having caught the disease while nursing him.

A sad day that was for the poor widower who was left with five motherless children to care for, and it is small wonder that he scarcely knew where to turn. While he was still dazed by his burden of grief, a stranger came to the desolate little home on the lake, and asked to see Mr. Farragut. He was Capt. Porter, the son of the old man who had been cared for in his last sickness by the Farraguts, and his son had come to express his gratitude for their kindness, and to offer to adopt one of the boys, as a token of appreciation, if Mr. Farragut was willing to give one up.

Although it meant final parting with his boy, and that was not easy, George Farragut felt it was a wise thing to do, and as his eldest son, William, was already in the navy, David was the next to accept the offered advantage. Captain Porter was at that time in command of the naval station at New Orleans, and his showy uniform made a great impression on little David, who though sad at leaving his father and brothers, was eager to go with this handsome new guardian, and as soon as the farewells were said, and his slender wardrobe was packed, Captain Porter took him away with him to his home in New Orleans, and from there to Washington where he was placed in a good school.

Farragut was a bright, intelligent boy, with an honest, pleasant face, and though he was short, he stood very erect and always held his head very high.

"I cannot afford to lose any of my inches," he always said.

One day he was introduced to the Secretary of the Navy, who after asking him many questions, was so delighted with the boy's quick answers that he patted him on the head, saying:

"My boy, when you are ten years old, I shall make you a midshipman in the navy."

That promise seemed too good to be true to young Farragut, who was then nine and a half years' old, but the Secretary of the Navy did not forget it but kept his word, and

FARRAGUT

the appointment came promptly, putting the boy in a seventh heaven of anticipation. Then the arrangement was made that he was to go with Capt. Porter, and on that October day of 1812 when the *Essex* sailed out of the Delaware river, the young midshipman stood in all his proud splendour of uniform beside the Captain who was already his ideal of a naval hero.

For several months the *Essex* cruised about in the Atlantic, during which time Captain Porter was able to capture some English vessels, among them the *Alert,* and the *Essex* was crowded with prisoners taken from the prize ships.

One night when young Farragut lay apparently asleep, but in reality listening and watching, the coxswain of the *Alert* came to his hammock with a pistol in hand. Farragut scarcely breathed until he had passed by, then noiselessly the young midshipman crept to the cabin where Captain Porter was, aroused him and told him what he had seen. The Captain sprang from his cot, crying "Fire! Fire!" The sailors rushed on deck at the cry, and the rebels were in irons almost before they knew what had happened, while to young Farragut belonged the credit of having averted a mutiny.

Months passed, and still Captain Porter had not been able to find the American squadron, so he decided to make a trip around Cape Horn, and cruise about on the Pacific, which decision pleased young Farragut, as he was eager for an experience of real sea life. And he certainly had it. The weather was bitterly cold, and for twenty-one days the ship was lashed by terrific gales, by the end of which time the provisions were almost gone, and each man had only a small daily allowance of bread and water, which was not a light experience, with appetites whetted by salt air and hard work. After rounding the cape, Captain Porter sailed north along the west coast of South America and stopped at an island near the coast of Chili, and here all the sailors went ashore with their guns, and killed some wild hogs and horses, and even the horse-flesh they ate with keen relish, after being so long without fresh meat. Then for months they cruised about in the Pacific, and as he had done in the Atlantic cruise, so in the Pacific, Captain Porter captured several English vessels and also warned some American whaling ships of danger. These had been at sea for so long that they had not even heard of the war. Every now and again the *Essex* stopped at an island where the sailors could kill seals, or when they anchored in a bay, they fished for cod, and at one island where they stayed for quite a while, they found prickly pears to eat, and killed pigeons which the cook on the *Essex* made into pies, and turtles which they caught were made into soup, and the salt air and the free vigorous life gave them all ravenous appetites, and young Farragut felt the keenest joy of living which he had ever experienced.

On that island where they stayed so long they found a curious post-office—a link connecting whoever should discover it with the outer world of passing men and vessels. It was just a box nailed to a tree, where messages or letters could be left to be picked up by other vessels which happened to be going in the right direction to carry them.

A far cry indeed from that island post-box to the wireless stations of to-day, flashing news from sea to land—from land to sea!

At last in May, 1813, the *Essex* sailed away from the island, and soon more English vessels were sighted and captured. One of these prizes Captain Porter wished to have taken to Valparaiso, and as through all the long cruise

FARRAGUT

he had kept a watchful eye on young Farragut, he now determined to put the boy's ability to a hard test.

Farragut was then only twelve years old, just think of it,—twelve years old, but the Captain put him in charge of the captured vessel, while its grey-haired old captain was required to navigate it to Valparaiso under Farragut's command.

The charge of such a vessel on such a trip was no light matter for a boy to undertake, and Farragut's joy and pride fairly oozed from every inch of his alert figure, beamed from every feature of his face. The old captain of the ship, in none too good a humour at having been captured by the Americans, was still more angry at being obliged to take orders from a mere child, and tried to ignore him, but as Farragut paid no heed to his snubs, he tried a different method. When Farragut gave orders that " the maintopsail be filled away," the captain answered that he would shoot any man who dared to touch a rope without his orders, and then went below to get his pistols. There wasn't a moment to lose. Instantly Farragut called one of his men, and told him what had happened and what he wanted done, and his frank manner and words accomplished what no amount of commands would have done.

"Aye, aye, sir!" answered the faithful seaman, and at once prepared to obey the order, while Farragut sent down word to the rebellious captain not to come on deck with a pistol if he did not wish to go overboard.

There was no question from that moment as to who was master of the vessel, while the boy was greatly admired for his bravery which had been equal to such an emergency, and the vessel was brought safely into port by the young commander, who then went back to the *Essex,* proud in the fact of having accomplished the task assigned him.

On his return, Captain Porter had decided to go at

once to some islands far out in the Pacific, where he could refit the *Essex,* and so they sailed in that direction, and when near the islands they were sighted by some of the natives who paddled out in a canoe to meet them, and eagerly invited the sailors ashore, promising them fruit and other provisions. The natives were indeed a strange sight to the eyes of the American boys, for their bodies were heavily tattooed, and gaily ornamented with feathers in true barbaric fashion, but they were very friendly and during the six weeks while the ship was being refitted, although the American sailors were given lessons daily by the chaplain of the *Essex,* when the lesson was over, they were allowed to mingle freely with the islanders, and Farragut learned many new things from them, things which were afterwards invaluable to him. To the islanders, swimming was as natural and as easy as walking, and although David never became as proficient in this as his new friends, still he learned to swim easily and fast, and too, they taught him how to walk on stilts, and how to use a spear with skill and ease, and in such sports and occupations, time passed quickly and the Americans were most regretful when the day came for them to say farewell to their island friends. But the *Essex* was ready to sail for Valparaiso, so off they went and when they sailed away, young Farragut was almost as much developed in muscle, and as bronzed by the sun and wind, as were the friends he left behind him on that island to which he always looked back as an enchanted land.

Two months later when the *Essex* was lying quietly at anchor in the harbour of Valparaiso, and many of her crew happened to be on shore, two English war vessels bore swiftly down upon the *Essex* in a very menacing way, and Captain Porter was afraid they would attack him, which they had no right to do, for Chili was not at war with either

FARRAGUT

England or America, and so an American vessel should have been safe within that port.

One of these English vessels was a frigate called *The Phoebe* and the other a sloop named *The Cherub*. The *Phoebe* passed within fifteen feet of the *Essex*, when Captain Porter, who was standing on deck, hailed her, saying:

"If you touch a single yardarm I shall board you instantly!"

The *Phoebe* passed by without a reply and then both English vessels anchored at the entrance of the harbour, by doing which they kept the *Essex* a prisoner. In this position the vessels remained for several weeks, when there was a tremendous gale, in which the cables of the *Essex* gave way, and she at once began to drift towards the English ships. Captain Porter decided that this was his chance to escape, and setting all sail he made for the open sea.

Suddenly something snapped. Down crashed the main topmast, carrying sails, rigging and even some of the crew into the water. In such a crippled condition escape was impossible, and the *Essex* was driven back again to shore, where she was brought to anchor within pistol shot of the beach.

The *Essex* had only four guns that could shoot as far as the cannon of the English. The *Phoebe* and the *Cherub* took a position out of range of almost all of the guns of the *Essex*, and then poured broadside after broadside into the unfortunate American.

For two hours and a half the battle raged, the *Phoebe* throwing seven hundred eighteen-pound shots at the *Essex*. Captain Porter and his crew fought bravely until one hundred and twenty-four of their men had been killed or wounded and during all this terrible battle, the first which David Farragut had ever seen, there was no braver officer on the ship than the little midshipman, who hurried here and there, carrying messages for the captain, bringing powder for the guns, and helping wherever he was needed. Years later in discussing this scene, Farragut said:

"I shall never forget the horrid impression made upon me at the sight of the first man I had ever seen killed. It staggered me at first, but they soon began to fall so fast that it all appeared like a dream, and produced no effect on my nerves. . . . Some gun-primers were wanted and I was sent after them. In going below, while I was on the ward-room ladder, the Captain of the gun directly opposite the hatchway was struck full in the face by an eighteen pound shot, and fell back on me. We tumbled down the hatch together. I lay for some moments stunned by the blow, but soon recovered consciousness enough to rush up on deck. The Captain seeing me covered with blood, asked if I were wounded, to which I replied, 'I believe not, sir.'

"'Then,' said he, 'where are the primers?' This brought me to my senses and I ran below again and brought up the primers."

When Captain Porter had been forced to surrender, the wounded men were carried to shore, and young Farragut volunteered his services to help the surgeons, and worked tirelessly, rolling bandages and waiting on the injured men, whose admiration he won by his devoted service; and so pleased was Captain Porter with his bravery throughout the whole battle, that he mentioned it in his official despatches to the government. Farragut himself in speaking of the battle later said:

"I never earned Uncle Sam's money so faithfully."

All of the American prisoners of war were put on board an unarmed vessel, and made to promise that they

FARRAGUT

would not take up arms against the English until they had been exchanged for an equal number of English prisoners, after giving which promise the *Essex* was allowed to sail for the United States. When Farragut, the plucky little midshipman was taken on board the prison-ship, tears of mortification rolled down his cheeks.

"Never mind, my little fellow," said the Captain, "perhaps it will be your turn next."

"I hope so," was David's answer and his tears turned into a smile as he saw "Murphy" his pet pig being brought on board, and at once rushed to claim him, but the English sailors refused to allow that it was his, saying:

"You are a prisoner and your pig too."

"We always respect private property," answered David, seizing hold of the sailors, and of Murphy, with unyielding determination, and after a vigorous tussle he won his beloved pig.

Now prisoners of war, the Captain and crew of the *Essex* arrived in the harbour of New York on July 7th, 1814, and young Farragut, while waiting to be exchanged, went to Captain Porter's home at Chester, Pa., and while there was under the tuition of a Mr. Neif, a quaint instructor who had been one of Napoleon's celebrated Guards. He gave the boys in his care no lessons from books, but taught them about plants and animals and how to climb, taking long walks with them and giving them military drills as well, all of which Farragut enjoyed.

In the following November, the English and Americans, having made an exchange of prisoners, Farragut was free to return to the navy, but as a treaty of peace was made only a few weeks later between the Americans and English, he did not have to serve against the latter again, and during the next two years he made only one short uneventful cruise, being quartered the rest of the time on a receiving ship, or a vessel stationed at the navy yards, where recruits are received into the service.

But in the Spring of 1816, he went on a cruise which proved most interesting, on the *Washington,* a beautiful new ship carrying seventy-four guns, which was to take the American minister to Naples. Before leaving for the cruise, the President of the United States, James Madison, visited the *Washington,* and among his suite was Captain Porter, then a naval commissioner, who had come to say good-bye to the boy whom he loved devotedly.

Farragut was sad to say good-bye, but full too of the desire for change and adventure, and the new trip was a great experience for him.

The *Washington* cruised all summer in the Mediterranean, stopping at many places, which gave Farragut an opportunity to study geography in the finest way possible. The great volcano Vesuvius was in eruption when he visited it, which was an experience he never forgot, and another of a very different kind was when the King of Naples and the Emperor of Austria visited the *Washington* and were entertained with great display and elegance. After stopping at the coast towns of Tunis, Tripoli and Algiers, the *Washington* finally put up for the winter in a Spanish harbour, and then, as during the entire cruise, the boys were taught by the ship's chaplain, Mr. Folsom, who was so devoted to David that when in the fall of 1817 he was appointed consul to Tunis, he wrote to the Captain of the *Washington* asking permission to take the boy with him, because, he said to the commodore " he is entirely destitute of the aids of fortune and the influence of friends, other than those whom his character may attach to him," and the request was granted.

FARRAGUT

Farragut spent nine delightful and valuable months with his old friend, who gave the boy every opportunity, not only for study, but to gain such polish and worldly experience as he would need in later life and David eagerly profited by every advantage given him. Then the Danish consul, who was also an admirer of the bright sturdy boy, invited him to visit him. Farragut was now sixteen years old, and it was at that time that the first real hardship of his life came to him, when as the result of a sunstroke, his eyes were weakened, and never entirely recovered.

Soon it was time for him to go on duty on the *Washington* again, and Mr. Folsom, tearful with regret at being obliged to part from the boy, took him in his arms and gave him his blessing and their paths in life parted, although forty years later, when Farragut had become a famous Admiral he sent a token of respect and love to Mr. Folsom, showing that he had never forgotten his old friend.

When Farragut was eighteen years old, he was called to America to take his examination for a lieutenancy, which he took and passed successfully, but as there was no vacancy just then in the navy, he was obliged to wait, and although he spent the time happily with the Porters in their Virginia home, he was glad indeed when the chance came to cruise again, for he was a thorough sailor, and the love of the sea ran hot in his veins.

For years both the American and English had been waging war against bands of pirates who infested the coast of the West Indies. These robbers had small fast ships, and would attack unarmed merchantmen, seize all the valuable they could carry away or destroy, and sometimes kill the crew or put them ashore on some desert island. Ever since peace with England had been declared, Captain Porter had been a commissioner of the navy, and made no sea voyages, but now he offered to resign this position and attempt to drive the pirates away, only demanding that the government should give him a fleet of small vessels which could follow the pirates into their retreats.

The government accepted his offer, and gave him orders to fit out such a fleet as he chose, and he bought eight small schooners, similiar to those used by the pirates, and also five large row-boats or barges, which were called the "mosquito fleet" and Farragut was assigned to one of the vessels named the *Greyhound,* and in command of it he had many exciting encounters with the pirates. At one time when off the Southern coast of Cuba, some of the *Greyhound's* crew who had gone ashore to hunt game, were fired on by the pirates, and returned this fire without effect, then went back to their ship. Farragut was ordered to take a party of men to capture the pirates, and at three o'clock the next morning, they set out in the barges, and after landing on the island, had no easy time to find the pirate camp, as they had to cut their way through thickets of trailing vines, thorny bushes and cactus plants and in such intense heat that some of the men fainted from exhaustion. They found the camp, but their prey had fled! Evidently the approaching vessels had been seen, and the pirates were gone. The sailors at once searched their camp, which was protected by several cannon, and there they found some houses a hundred feet long, and also an immense cave filled with all kinds of goods taken from plundered vessels.

The sailors burned the houses, and carried off the plunder and the cannon to their boats, while David carried away a monkey as his prize. Just as the men were returning to their boats, they heard a great noise behind them, and

FARRAGUT

thought surely that the pirates had come back to attack them, and Farragut stood still and made a speech to the sailors, urging them to fight bravely and to stand their ground like men. Imagine their surprise and amusement when they found their foes were not pirates, but thousands of land-crabs scurrying through the briars!

This was only one of the incidents that young Farragut had while on his first cruise as acting lieutenant. During the entire cruise to the West Indies, the American sailors suffered much from yellow fever and from exposure, and in alluding to the voyage in after days, Farragut said:

"I never owned a bed during my cruise in the West Indies, but laid me down to rest wherever I found the most comfortable berth."

The pirates were finally driven from the seas, their boats burned or captured, and their camps entirely destroyed, and Farragut's first and most exciting cruise as a youthful commander came to an end. The honours which were his at a later day were such as come to the man of years of training and experience, but from the day when the little midshipman stood on the deck of the *Essex* beside Captain Porter as she sailed down the Delaware river, to the time when he stood in the proud glory of his title, the first admiral of America, his is the story of a man who won his fame by a never varying attention to detail, a never ending effort for self-improvement, and a never relaxed adherence to duty.

All honour to Midshipman Farragut—the Admiral-to-be!

MOZART:
The Boy Musician

MOZART:
The Boy Musician

JOHANNES CHRYSOSTEMUS WOLFGANGUS THEOPHILUS MOZART—what a burden to be put upon a baby's tiny shoulders!

If there is any truth underlying the belief that a name can in some measure foreshadow a child's future, then surely Wolfgang Mozart, who was born in Salzburg in 1756, came honestly by his heritage of greatness, for when he was only a day old he received the five-part name, to which was later added his confirmation name of Sigismundus. But as soon as he could choose for himself, the little son of Marianne and Leopold Mozart from his store of names, selected Wolfgang, to which he added Amadeus, by which combination he was always known, and the name is for ever linked with the memory of a great genius.

Almost before he could talk plainly the little fellow showed himself to be a musical prodigy, and when he was scarcely three years old he would steal into the room where his father was giving a lesson on the harpsichord to Anna (or "Nannerl," as she was called), the sister five years older than himself, and while she was being taught, Wolfgang would listen and watch with breathless attention.

One day when the lesson was over, he begged his father to teach him too, but Leopold Mozart only laughed as he answered, glancing down into the child's serious face looking so intently into his:

"Wait, my little man, thou art but a baby yet. Wait

awhile, my Wolferl!" and the disappointed little musician crept away, but as soon as Nannerl and his father had left the room, the tiny fellow crept back again, went to the harpsichord and standing on tiptoe, touched the keys with his chubby fingers stretched wide apart until he reached and played *a perfect chord!* Leopold Mozart was in another part of the house, but his sensitive ear caught the sound, and he rushed back to find his baby on tiptoe before the harpsichord, giving the first hint of his marvellous ability.

At once the proud and excited father began to give him lessons, and always, too, from that day, whenever Nannerl had her lesson, Wolfgang perched on his father's knee, and listened with rapt absorption, and often when the lesson was over, he would repeat what she had played in exact imitation of her manner of playing.

Leopold Mozart, who was himself a talented musician, saw with pride almost beyond expression, that both of his children inherited his musical ability, and soon felt that Wolfgang was a genius. When the boy was only four, his father, to test his powers, tried to teach him some minuets which to his perfect astonishment, Wolfgang played after him in a most extraordinary manner, not merely striking the notes correctly, but marking the rhythm with accurate expression, and to learn and play each minuet the little fellow required only half an hour.

When he was five years old, one day his father entered the sitting-room of their home and found Wolfgang bending over a table, writing so busily that he did not hear his father enter, or see that he was standing beside him. Wolfgang's chubby little hand held the pen awkwardly, but held it with firm determination while it travelled back and forth across a large sheet of paper on which he was scribbling a

MOZART

strange collection of hieroglyphics, with here and there a huge blot, testifying to his haste and inexperience in the use of ink.

What was he trying to do? His father's curiosity finally overcame him and he asked:

"What are you doing, Wolfgang?" The curly head was raised with an impatient gesture.

"I am composing a concerto for the harpsichord. I have nearly finished the first part."

"Let me see it."

'No, please, I have not yet finished."

But even as he spoke, the eager father had taken up the paper and carried it over to where a friend stood, and they looked it over together, exchanging amused glances at the queer characters on it. Presently Leopold Mozart, after looking carefully at it, said:

"Why it really seems to be composed by rule! But it is so difficult that no one could ever play it."

"Oh, yes, they could, but it must be studied first," exclaimed little Wolfgang eagerly, and running to the harpsichord, he added:

"See, this is the way it begins," and he was able to play enough of it, to show what his idea in writing it had been, and his father and the friend who had before exchanged glances of amusement, now looked at each other with wonder not untouched with awe.

In the Mozart collection at Salzburg, there is still preserved a music book in which those early pieces written by little Wolfgang were written down by his father, and also the minuets he learned, and in the book his father wrote after them:

"The preceding minuets were learnt by Wolfgang in his fourth year," and further on we find the record:

TEN BOYS FROM HISTORY

"This minuet and trio Wolfgang learned in half an hour on the 26th day of January, 1761, the day before his fifth birthday, at half-past nine at night."

In his first composition the sense of perfect form is felt to a remarkable degree, and the little book in which it was written down, not only accompanied the family on their travels, but in it Wolfgang also wrote down his first sonatas, published in 1763.

When he was not much over five years old, Wolfgang was chosen to take the part of chorister in a Latin comedy which was given at the close of the school year of the Salzburg Gymnasium, and among the one hundred and fifty young people who took part in the entertainment one can picture the charming little musical fellow as the great feature of the occasion, and many stories were told at that time of his marvellous sense of sound, and the ease with which he overcame every technical difficulty. Meanwhile he learned to play on the violin, and could tell, it is said, when one violin was an eighth of a tone lower than another. Even games, to be interesting to him, had to be accompanied by music, and a family friend in writing of him says: "If he and I carried playthings from one room to another, the one who went empty-handed must sing, and play a march on the violin as he walked."

On an evening when a number of violinists were gathered in the Mozart home to play together, Wolfgang, who had recently been learning to play the violin, begged to play with them. His father refused to let him, and told him to run away, but the second violinist called him back, saying:

"Never mind, little man; wipe away those tears and stand by me." So close beside him stood the little chap, and presently all were surprised to hear a clear, clean-cut tone coming from the child's violin. His touch was so ex-

MOZART

quisite, his interpretation so masterly, that presently the second violinist laid down his instrument and listened breathlessly, while Wolfgang played on and on, forgetful of everything but the magic spell of the music, and as his father listened, his heart throbbed with pride and joy, and tears rolled down his face, as he exclaimed:

"Little music-king thou art, my Wolferl, and thou shalt reign over us all!"

From that moment it was plain that Wolfgang Mozart was a musical prodigy, and as little Nannerl, too, had great talent, the proud father now determined to show them to a world which was ever eager to applaud such genius, and in 1762 he made his first experiment of taking the children on a concert tour. This was so successful that before Wolfgang was eight years old and Nannerl twelve, they had appeared at the Courts of Vienna, Paris, Munich and London, and everywhere Wolfgang made friends with rich and poor alike, his personality was so full of charm and simple dignity.

Once, during their travels, being detained by a heavy shower at Ypps, they took refuge in a monastery. The monks were at supper and did not know of the arrival of any stranger, until suddenly from the chapel came wonderful music, music grave and gay, sad, sweet, thrilling, and marvellous in its appeal to hearts and souls. The Fathers were frightened, not knowing who could have entered their sanctuary, thinking it must be a spirit, when at last a light was brought, and creeping into the chapel, they discovered little Wolfgang at the organ, not a vision, but just a mortal boy. The Fathers were overcome with amazement and lavished all possible courtesies on the wonderful little musician and his family while they remained.

On entering Vienna, at the Custom House, Wolfgang,

after a brief chat with the official there, took out his violin, and played to the official, who was so delighted with the boy and his music, that the family had no trouble with examination of their luggage, as they would otherwise have had.

The Imperial family of Vienna were all very fond of music, and had also had their curiosity greatly excited in regard to this child prodigy, so it was not strange that only a few days after the Mozarts arrived, Leopold should have received a command to bring his children to play at Schoenbrum, an imperial palace near Vienna, and this without any effort on Mozart's part to get the invitation.

The Emperor was delighted with the little "sorcerer" as he called Wolfgang, and besides listening to his real playing with deepest interest, he made him play with one finger, in which the little fellow was perfectly successful. Then he asked him to play with the keys covered by a piece of cloth, which he did instantly, and these musical tricks suggested by the Emperor's fancy, thereafter formed a far from unimportant part of Wolfgang's repertoire on his long concert tours, and always interested his audiences. The boy had a keen sense of humour, and always entered heartily into any joke that was made with him, but sometimes he could be very serious, as for instance, when he was called to play for the court composer, George Wagenseil, who was himself a proficient performer on the harpsichord. The Emperor stepped back when Wagenseil same forward, and Mozart said very seriously to him:

"I play a concerto by you, you must turn over the pages for me," and turn the pages the great man did.

The Emperor ordered one hundred ducats to be paid to Wolfgang's father for the performance, and the Empress,

MOZART

both then and later, was kindness itself to both the children, and sent them expensive and beautiful clothes. In writing to a friend at that time, Leopold Mozart said:

"Would you like to know what Wolferl's dress is like? It is the finest cloth, lilac-coloured, the best of moiré of the same colour. Coat and top-coat with a double broad border of gold."

In the portrait which is in the Mozart collection in Salzburg, Mozart is painted in this dress, and he wore it with as much ease as if he had always been used to such finery. Also he never showed any embarrassment or self-consciousness when in the presence of royalty, and once jumped on the lap of the Empress, Maria Theresa, put his arms around her neck and kissed her as effusively as if she had been his mother, while he treated the princesses as if they were his sisters. Marie Antoinette was one of his great favourites after she helped him up from a severe fall on a highly polished floor. To her great amusement he thanked her by saying:

"You are good. I will marry you," and when the Crown Prince Joseph, who afterwards became Emperor, played the violin before the little prodigy, he exclaimed: "Fie!" at something he did not like, then, "that was false!" at another bar, and finally applauded, with cries of "Bravo!"

Little Nannerl who played only less well than her remarkable brother, was a charmingly pretty, piquant little girl, whose manner, both in society and in the concert hall, was winning and demure, while Wolfgang's grace and elegance of manner were striking. Wherever the children went, people went mad over them. They were the fashion, the furore, no musical entertainment was a success without them, and they were so petted that they might easily have been spoiled, had it not been for their father's wise and watchful care. But with true German caution, the father guarded them from bad effects of over-excitement or indulgence. All sorts of presents were constantly given them, among which were many jewels and beautiful articles of clothing, but the clothes were only used on concert nights or special occasions, the jewellery was kept locked up in a box, and the children were only allowed to see or handle it when they had been especially good.

When Paris was the headquarters of the travellers, all possible honour was given them, and the concerts in the French capital brought the Mozarts a substantial sum and they were received very kindly in a visit to the Court of Versailles; of which visit little Nannerl said later, that her only recollection was of the Marquise de Pompadour standing Wolfgang on a table, that he wanted to kiss her, and when she drew back, he said indignantly:

"Who is she that she will not let me kiss her? The Empress kissed me."

The King's daughters were very kind to the children, and on New Year's Day, 1764, the Mozart family dined with the royal family. Wolfgang sat next to the Queen, who talked to him in German, translating the conversation to Louis Fifteenth, while near Wolfgang sat his father and his mother, and Nannerl sat on the opposite side of the table by the Dauphin.

After playing at Versailles the little musicians became the fashion in Paris, and every circle was open to them, while Wolfgang's reputation as a musical genius was steadily growing, and he had already composed two sonatas which were really good pieces of work from an artistic point of view.

Leaving Paris at last, the Mozarts arrived in London,

MOZART

and after taking lodgings, they hastened to adopt English customs.

"How do you suppose," wrote Leopold Mozart, to a friend, "my wife and girl look in English hats, and the great Wolfgang in English clothes?"

Almost immediately they were requested to play at Buckingham House, before the King and Queen, where they met with exceptional kindness and appreciation, and the London visit was an unqualified success, one brilliant performance following another in quick succession, until it seemed as if the quaint, charming little music-king who made such an imposing appearance on the stage, must be really as old and grown-up as he seemed when playing in public.

But while they were in England, in lodgings in Chelsea, which was then open country, Leopold Mozart was very ill for a time, so the children could not practise, and for awhile were obliged to run wild, and it would have been hard to imagine that the bright little German girl and the pretty boy, busy making houses and grottos and arbours out of stones and earth and leaves, at the rear of their lodgings, were the infant prodigies of the concert stage. But even then, while he could not use the harpsichord, little Wolfgang was composing, and when tired of out-of-door sports would sit down, with his sister beside him and work on a symphony for the orchestra, and it was thus that his earliest symphonies were composed, which were all marked by real artistic form and feeling. The chief advantage of these compositions, however, was that Wolfgang kept in practise, and was able to announce that at his next concerts all the instrumental numbers would be his own compositions, which, of course, made a great impression on his audiences.

Again they were invited to Court, but this time Leopold Mozart felt obliged to have six sonatas of Wolfgang's for harpsichord and violin, printed and dedicated to the Queen, so the visit was not the financial benefit to the Mozarts that the first one had been, and from that time the concert tour brought in less great returns than those of the previous months, for both Nannerl and Wolfgang were seriously sick. But they recovered and journeyed on to Holland, where Wolfgang was called to play before the Prince of Orange, and commanded to write six sonatas for the princess, also to write a variation for the harpsichord on the melody which is sung, played and whistled by everybody in Holland and is the real Duch national hymn.

The little composer was also called upon for various other pieces of musical work and in no way disappointed his critics or his audiences. Again the trio journeyed on, stopping wherever the father felt that his son's fame might be increased by a concert.

To Paris they went again, then through France to Switzerland, and finally journeyed homeward, reaching Salzburg in November of 1766, and it was a matter of great interest to their friends to find the children who had left home three years ago, still happy, hearty boy and girl, despite all their new worldly experience.

Old and young came to bid them welcome, to hear the story of their adventures, and to see the numerous and costly presents, about which they had heard so much. They found pretty Nannerl prettier than ever, and Wolfgang, notwithstanding the severe illness he had recently had, looked normally well and happy, and was as childish in his interests as if he had not become a public idol.

It is said that at that time, so glad was he to be at home again, that he rode merrily around the room on his father's

MOZART

stick, as he had done three years before, and played with his favourite cat just as he used to do, the cat having been well cared for in the absence of the family, by a friend.

During their tour Wolfgang had created for himself an imaginary kingdom, which he called Rücken. This country was to be inhabited entirely by children, and he was to be the king. His idea of the place was so distinct that a friend had to draw him a map of the cities in it, to which he gave names, and his friends were completely fascinated to hear him talk of his droll conceits, when he was not holding them spell-bound by the magic of his music.

And now as soon as they were settled down again in their home, Leopold Mozart began to instruct Wolfgang seriously in counterpoint, that he might be thoroughly fitted for his life-work, and then as his precocious childhood begins to merge into young boyhood, we find him working indefatigably, working with fingers and with brain, every faculty alert, to conquer technique and achieve perfection in his art.

In the summer of 1767, when Mozart was eleven, they started on a new tour, for which the little prodigy composed four pianoforte concerti, which were interesting on account of certain harmonic effects produced in them, but that second tour, was not a fortunate one, for during it, both Nannerl and Wolfgang were stricken with small-pox, which took a very violent form, and poor Wolfgang lay blind for nine days, and convalescence was slow, and hard to bear. Again they visited Vienna, but there they found things greatly changed, for while in former days, music was always a feature of great social gatherings, now the only pleasure seemed to be in balls, and there was absolutely no interest shown in Mozart, the child prodigy. Also much jealousy was shown towards the Mozarts by other musicians, and when Wolfgang set to work on an opera, to be used with the text written for him by the Viennese dramatic poet of the day, and had already completed a score of six hundred and fourteen pages, it was said that Wolfgang had not written it at all, that it was his father's composition. To contradict these statements, in the presence of several prominent critics, Leopold opened a volume of Metastatio, at the first aria, which he placed in front of Wolfgang, and before that assemblage of critical older men, the boy seized a pen and wrote without hesitation, music to the aria for several instruments, and with such incredible swiftness that the company watching him were dumb with amazement at his ability.

But matters did not grow brighter—all sorts of unpleasant incidents occurred to embitter the tourists, and at the end of a year the family returned once again to Salzburg.

At that time Italy was the Mecca of the musician, and to study and win his first laurels there was the ideal of every musical student. The musical atmosphere of Salzburg was narrow and provincial, and Leopold Mozart wished Wolfgang to escape from it, so presently we find young Mozart and his father journeying Southward to Italy where Wolfgang is studying, meeting interesting people, playing in public, and writing amusing letters home to Nannerl, who was becoming more devoted to her home duties now, than to her music, but even so it was always into her ears that Wolfgang poured his musical feelings, sure that he would be understood.

When he was in Rome, he saw in the Sistine chapel the painting of "The Last Judgment," while listening to the wonderful music of "The Miserere," which music is only performed in Holy Week by the Pope's choir, and no one

MOZART

has ever been allowed to have a copy of the music or even to see it. But so accurate was little Mozart's memory, that after leaving the chapel, he not only wrote out the music correctly, but could also sing it perfectly, a feat which made him the musical marvel of his age!

For two years he worked and studied, and accomplished great things musically, then the Elector of Bavaria invited him to write a comic opera for the Carnival, which invitation the boy joyfully accepted, and at once set to work on the none too easy task. He was now at home again, and his father and Nannerl listened eagerly to his themes, as bit by bit he elaborated them.

In due time the opera was finished; it was called "La Finta Giardiniera," and Wolfgang, accompanied by his father and pretty sister, set off for Munich, where the performance was to be given, where court life was very gay just then, and where Nannerl and Wolfgang were sure to have much to amuse and interest them.

Nannerl was taken to board by a widow who lived in the old market-place, while Leopold and the young composer were obliged to take rooms nearer the Court. At once rehearsals of the opera began, and the days were marked by a succession of exciting events for Wolfgang and for Nannerl, into whose apartment Wolfgang ran half a dozen times a day to report progress.

Up and down the street, humming bits of the opera or intent on some new scenic effect, dashed the young composer a dozen times a day, and he and Nannerl were perfectly sure that no performance ever was or ever could be so marvellous, as this one was to be.

At last the great night came. Nannerl was dressed in her dainty white gown hours before the time, but Wolfgang, who was detained at the opera house until the last moment, had just time to jump into his fine new costume of satin and lace, with the flash of brilliants in his ruff and on his slippers; without a glance in the mirror, but he looked like a proud young prince when he joined his father and sister, although the hand that he slipped through Nannerl's arm was trembling. Who could say what the evening would hold of triumph or of failure? No wonder he trembled.

When they arrived at the opera house, it was crowded to the doors. All the court was there in gala dress, but the youthful music-master, scarcely nineteen years old then, sat with his father and Nannerl, unmindful that all eyes were focussed on him, forgetful of all but the performance of his opera.

The music began, and from the first note to the last, the opera was a triumphant success. Young Mozart then became the object of the wildest enthusiasm, and from that moment his popularity as a musician was established.

There let us leave him, as he stands before us in his stately costume, bowing acknowledgment of the applause raining upon him, with the blaze of light shining full upon his clean-cut dignified face, and when we hear his famous compositions played, let us think back to that night of his first great public triumph, when he was nineteen years old.

Pianist, violinist, composer, little music-king and great genius as well—the world owes a debt of gratitude to Wolfgang Amadeus Mozart, which can only be paid in the coin of appreciation.

HELPING YOUR CHILDREN CHOOSE THEIR HEROES THROUGH READING

by

Adam Starchild

Children today are starved for the image of real heroes. Celebrities are not the same thing as heroes. Heroes existed way before celebrities ever did, even though celebrities now outshine heroes in children's consciousness.

Worshiping celebrities leaves children with a distinctly empty feeling -- it doesn't teach that they'll have to make sacrifices if they want to achieve anything worthwhile. No-talents become celebrities all the time. The result is that people don't seem to care about achievement or talent -- fame is the only objective.

What is a hero? Despite immense differences in cultures, heroes around the world generally share a number of traits that instruct and inspire people. A hero does something worth talking about, but a hero goes beyond mere fame or celebrity. The hero lives a life worthy of imitation. If they serve only their own fame, they may be celebrities but not heroes. Heroes are catalysts for change. They create new possibilities. They have a vision, and the skill and charm to implement their vision.

TEN BOYS FROM HISTORY

Heroes may also be fictional. Children may identify with a character because of the values projected. People tend to grow to be like the people that they admire, but if a child never has any heroes what images will he copy? Adults need heroes too, but the need is even more urgent for children because they don't know how to think abstractly. But they can imagine what their hero would do in the circumstances, and it gives them a useful reference point to build abstract thinking skills.

Good reading selections can help your children find their own heroes -- to provide the emotional experience of admiring a figure they can look up to. Through the wide variety of reading experiences and choices of heroes, your children will find those models that best suit them.

It is important that children become familiar with worthy examples -- both real and fictional -- that they can emulate.

This does not mean that everything they read needs to be populated with heroes. Children will turn away from fictional villains they don't like. It is important to avoid children's stories in which the hero commits and gets away with evil actions. Don't assume that because a story is traditional it is automatically the literature you want your child to read. It is easy to think "that's o.k., it's a traditional children's story and I know it isn't dirty" without giving a moment's thought to the other messages that the story might be subconsciously conveying to your child.

Goldilocks and the Three Bears is certainly a traditional story, and most parents buy the book almost automatically, without a thought to the message. Goldilocks is lost and frightened, goes to a house and knocks, but no one is home. But that doesn't justify the crimes that follow. Yes, crimes! Breaking and entering, petty vandalism and theft -- even the nerve to go to sleep in a bed which doesn't belong to her either.

AFTERWORD

Is this really what you intended to teach your child -- that if you get lost it is alright to break into anybody's house and use their property? The story may be traditional, but these aren't the values you want to be teaching. It is so easy to assume that a well known book is okay, and select it for your child without even being aware of the subtle messages that it conveys -- messages that may be having far more influence on your child than you realize. After all, aren't you the one that told your child that this was a good book -- or read the story aloud? As your child is exposed to these traditional stories, you will want to take the time to explain the lessons in them. Without this guidance you may be unknowingly confusing the child. A child can also become confused when the villains in the story are likeable people who do evil.

Visible heroes today may be a bit harder to find and less dramatic, which is all the more reason to help your children start with the clear cut fictional heroes and then gradually transfer those learned ideals to the real world around them. There is no better place for a child to start than well-selected stories and novels where the hero has ability and integrity -- somebody who accomplishes an important, positive job.

All children start life with the same empty brain cells. What the adults around them put into those minds determines the resulting personalities. Stories -- whether heard or read -- are some of the most fundamental influences on a child.

One writer whose books are highly suitable for all ages is Robert Heinlein. He uses a science fiction format to deliver important messages, and it is often easier for a child to receive and understand the message when the setting is entirely unfamiliar and the characters and events can therefore be seen more clearly. For an older child you might want to start with *The Past Through Tomorrow*, a collection of his shorter stories. This lets the child break the

TEN BOYS FROM HISTORY

reading into distinct units. For younger children look for *Podkayne of Mars*, *Between Planets*, or *Have Spacesuit, Will Travel*.

If your child likes westerns, try some of the books by Louis L'Amour.

For preschoolers, any Dr. Seuss books. They may not be obvious as sources of heroes from an adult viewpoint, but from a small child's viewpoint they have characters that are easy to remember.

For the whole family, try *The Fire Hunter* by Jim Kjelgaard or *Girl Who Owned a City* by O. T. Nelson. And Heinlein's *The Rolling Stones* or *Farmer in the Sky*. Both are strong family books about future pioneers who have to solve problems for themselves. These heroes had to make themselves intelligent and capable to make a new, better life for themselves.

Don't dismiss heroes just because they are fictional. The power of creative imagination is one that is critically important to develop in children. When they learn to imagine with confidence and pleasure things they can't actually see, it is the first step towards conceptualization and abstract thinking -- important skills for handling adult challenges.

AFTERWORD

About the Author

Over the past 25 years, Adam Starchild has been the author of several dozen books, and hundreds of magazine articles, primarily on business and finance. His articles have appeared in a wide range of publications around the world.

Now semi-retired, he was the president of an international consulting group specializing in banking, finance and the development of new businesses, and director of a trust company.

Although this formidable testimony to expertise in his field, plus his current preoccupation with other books-in-progress, would not seem to leave time for a well-rounded existence, Starchild has won two Presidential Sports Awards and written several cookbooks, and is currently involved in a number of personal charitable projects.

His website is at http://www.adamstarchild.com/

www.ingramcontent.com/pod-product-compliance
Lightning Source LLC
Chambersburg PA
CBHW032110090426
42743CB00007B/307